Teen Addiction

Other Books of Related Interest:

Opposing Viewpoints Series

Juvenile Crime

Marijuana

Mental Illness

Popular Culture

Teen Drug Abuse

Current Controversies Series

Drug Abuse

Drug Legalization

At Issue Series

Antidepressants

Are Americans Overmedicated?

Does Advertising Promote Substance Abuse?

Drug Testing

Heroin

Legalizing Drugs

Prescription Drugs

Steroids

What Causes Addiction?

Teen Addiction

Jill Karson, Book Editor

616
.860083
T258a

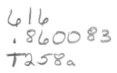

GREENHAVEN PRESS
An imprint of Thomson Gale, a part of The Thomson Corporation

THOMSON
GALE

Detroit • New York • San Francisco • New Haven, Conn. • Waterville, Maine • London

Christine Nasso, *Publisher*
Elizabeth Des Chenes, *Managing Editor*

© 2007 Thomson Gale, a part of The Thomson Corporation.

Thomson and Star logo are trademarks and Gale and Greenhaven Press are registered trademarks used herein under license.

For more information, contact:
Greenhaven Press
27500 Drake Rd.
Farmington Hills, MI 48331-3535
Or you can visit our Internet site at http://www.gale.com

LIBRARY OF CONGRESS CATALOGING-IN-PUBLICATION DATA

Teen addiction / Jill Karson, book editor.
    p. cm. -- (Contemporary issues companion)
  Includes bibliographical references and index.
  ISBN-13: 978-0-7377-3265-8 (lib. hardcover : alk. paper)
  ISBN-10: 0-7377-3265-2 (lib. hardcover : alk. paper)
  ISBN-13: 978-0-7377-3266-5 (pbk. : alk. paper)
  ISBN-10: 0-7377-3266-0 (pbk. : alk. paper)
  1. Teenagers--Substance use. 2. Drug addiction. I. Karson, Jill.
  HV4999.Y68T452 2007
  616.860083--dc22
                                                    2006021491

Printed in the United States of America
10 9 8 7 6 5 4 3 2 1

Contents

Chapter 3: Preventing and Treating Teen Addiction

Chapter 4: Personal Stories of Addiction and Recovery

Foreword

In the news, on the streets, and in neighborhoods, individuals are confronted with a variety of social problems. Such problems may affect people directly: A young woman may struggle with depression, suspect a friend of having bulimia, or watch a loved one battle cancer. And even the issues that do not directly affect her private life—such as religious cults, domestic violence, or legalized gambling—still impact the larger society in which she lives. Discovering and analyzing the complexities of issues that encompass communal and societal realms as well as the world of personal experience is a valuable educational goal in the modern world.

Effectively addressing social problems requires familiarity with a constantly changing stream of data. Becoming well informed about today's controversies is an intricate process that often involves reading myriad primary and secondary sources, analyzing political debates, weighing various experts' opinions—even listening to firsthand accounts of those directly affected by the issue. For students and general observers, this can be a daunting task because of the sheer volume of information available in books, periodicals, on the evening news, and on the Internet. Researching the consequences of legalized gambling, for example, might entail sifting through congressional testimony on gambling's societal effects, examining private studies on Indian gaming, perusing numerous Web sites devoted to Internet betting, and reading essays written by lottery winners as well as interviews with recovering compulsive gamblers. Obtaining valuable information can be time-consuming—since it often requires researchers to pore over numerous documents and commentaries before discovering a source relevant to their particular investigation.

Greenhaven's Contemporary Issues Companion series seeks to assist this process of research by providing readers with useful and pertinent information about today's complex issues. Each volume in this anthology series focuses on a topic of current interest, presenting informative and thought-provoking selections written from a wide variety of viewpoints. The readings selected by the editors include such diverse sources as personal accounts and case studies, pertinent factual and statistical articles, and relevant commentaries and overviews. This diversity of sources and views, found in every Contemporary Issues Companion, offers readers a broad perspective in one convenient volume.

In addition, each title in the Contemporary Issues Companion series is designed especially for young adults. The selections included in every volume are chosen for their accessibility and are expertly edited in consideration of both the reading and comprehension levels of the audience. The structure of the anthologies also enhances accessibility. An introductory essay places each issue in context and provides helpful facts such as historical background or current statistics and legislation that pertain to the topic. The chapters that follow organize the material and focus on specific aspects of the book's topic. Every essay is introduced by a brief summary of its main points and biographical information about the author. These summaries aid in comprehension and can also serve to direct readers to material of immediate interest and need. Finally, a comprehensive index allows readers to efficiently scan and locate content.

The Contemporary Issues Companion series is an ideal launching point for research on a particular topic. Each anthology in the series is composed of readings taken from an extensive gamut of resources, including periodicals, newspapers, books, government documents, the publications of private and public organizations, and Internet Web sites. In these volumes, readers will find factual support suitable for use in reports, debates, speeches, and research papers. The anthologies also facilitate further research, featuring a book and periodical bibliography and a list of organizations to contact for additional information.

A perfect resource for both students and the general reader, Greenhaven's Contemporary Issues Companion series is sure to be a valued source of current, readable information on social problems that interest young adults. It is the editors' hope that readers will find the Contemporary Issues Companion series useful as a starting point to formulate their own opinions about and answers to the complex issues of the present day.

Introduction

In Katherine Ketcham and Nicholas A. Pace's *Teens Under the Influence: The Truth About Kids, Alcohol, and Other Drugs—How to Recognize the Problem and What to Do About It*, one sixteen-year-old drug abuser states, "I can't even talk about drugs without wanting them. Man, my hands are sweating. I'm dying here. I mean it. I need my drugs. It's not even so much that I want them, because I want to quit using, I really do. It's just that I need them." The need is urgent, but as the young addict acknowledges, the impulse is not easily explained. Why are some teens prone to addiction while others—in fact the majority of youth—emerge from adolescence virtually untouched by problematic drug use or addiction? The answer is unclear. What is clear is that teens have vastly different experiences with alcohol, nicotine, and other drugs. Some teens, for example, will glide through adolescence avoiding drugs altogether, while others will seek every opportunity to experience the high of alcohol and other drugs. Likewise, not every teen who chooses to drink will become an alcoholic, nor will every teen who uses illicit drugs suffer serious consequences.

What, then, accounts for these differences? There is no blanket answer, but the question is widely studied—not only to pinpoint the causes of addiction but also to determine the scope of the problem and assess appropriate treatment and prevention strategies. Not surprisingly, research thus far has yielded wildly disparate conclusions. Most addiction experts agree, however, that certain genetic and environmental factors do appear to leave particular individuals more susceptible to chemical dependency and other forms of addiction. Opinion is divided, however, as to what extent addictive behaviors may be triggered by any given physiological, social, or environmental component.

According to addiction specialist Kenneth Blum, as quoted in Ketcham and Pace's book, "Psychological and sociological research indicates that the environment can trigger, worsen, or to some degree alleviate the genetic predisposition [to alcoholism and other drug addictions], but the determining factors are biogenetic and biochemical." Some of the current research appears to corroborate this view that addiction is largely determined by an individual's genetic makeup. Perhaps the most powerful evidence supporting a biological or genetic basis for addiction focuses on the brain reward centers of addicts. Children of alcoholics, for example, appear to have a diminished supply of receptors for dopamine, the neurotransmitter that gives people a sense of well-being. Teens with this inherited deficiency, then, may be more likely to ingest nicotine, alcohol, cocaine, or other drugs that temporarily boost their neurological pleasure system.

A related theory points to the unique brain chemistry of adolescents. Between the ages of ten and twenty-one, for example, the brain undergoes massive restructuring of its chemical and electrical circuitry. During this critical stage of neurological growth, adolescents appear to be particularly vulnerable to the effects of drugs. Addiction, consequently, progresses at a much faster rate. Similarly, thousands of other neurological differences, including a person's genetically determined temperament, may profoundly influence the course of addictive behaviors.

Other researchers assert that while these biological traits may predispose certain teens to problematic drug abuse, they do not tell the entire story. These experts point to a wide array of environmental and social factors—home life, school setting, cultural environment, and a variety of social pressures unique to the teen experience—that they believe are more likely to induce addictive behaviors. Many believe that the mass media offers a particularly striking example of how cultural influences shape teen behavior. As journalist and author

Kathiann M. Kowalski writes in a 2002 issue of *Current Health 2*, the tobacco industry, for instance, deliberately uses the media to attract adolescents to smoking—and perhaps lifelong addiction. Kowalski writes,

> Relatively few people start smoking or switch brands after age eighteen. So tobacco companies developed ad campaigns to lure teens. Themes included rugged independence, freedom, popularity, individuality, social acceptance, and carefree fun. Giveaways and promotional products became popular too. All these youth-appealing themes are still prominent in tobacco marketing.

Drugs, too, are readily available to most teens, and, depending on the environment that surrounds them, many will seek the opportunity to experiment. Adolescents undergoing the complex—and often tumultuous—stages of cognitive and emotional growth may find mind-altering chemicals particularly appealing. Stress, peer pressure, and family are all factors that shape the experiences of young people. Some teens are able to cope with the pressures of these factors; others are not. Experts suggest the list of at-risk youth may include children living in poverty; middle-class children stressed by grueling academic schedules and high parental expectations; teens who suffer mental or behavioral disorders including anxiety, depression, and attention-deficit disorders; and children who are not strongly connected to their families.

To journalist Meredith Maran, these and related factors that burden the social and psychological development of young people are most strongly correlated to addictive behaviors. As Maran writes in her book *Dirty: A Search for Answers Inside America's Teenage Drug Epidemic*, many teens will find in drugs a powerful antidote to their feelings of frustration, inadequacy, or hopelessness:

> When kids have a history of failure—in school, rehab, in their parent's eyes, in their peers', in their own—they see

only failure in their futures, if indeed they see futures for themselves at all. When kids feel hopeless, the prospect of staying sober can't compete with the instant gratification of getting high. If we want our kids to make choices that will benefit them (and all of us), we need to ensure that they experience and anticipate success in their lives early and often.

As Maran implies and evidence suggests, a strong and supportive family environment may, to some extent, inoculate youths from the risk factors that may lead to addiction. According to a report from the National Center on Addiction and Substance Abuse at Columbia University (CASA), parental engagement may be the most powerful weapon against substance abuse. In a 2005 newswire story, CASA's president, Joseph A. Califano Jr., commented on the paramount role of parents:

> There are no silver bullets—unfortunately, the tragedy of a child's substance abuse can strike any family; but one factor that does more to reduce teens' substance abuse risk than almost any other is parental engagement, and one of the simplest and most effective ways for parents to be engaged in their teens' lives is by having frequent family dinners. If I could wave a magic wand to make a dent in the substance abuse problem, I would make sure that every child in America had dinner with his or her parents at least five times a week. There is no more important thing a parent can do. Parental engagement in children's lives is the key to ridding our nation of the scourge of substance abuse.

While lack of parental involvement may be an unresolved problem for many at-risk youth, researchers have reported some encouraging trends in the statistical analysis of teen addiction. According to the University of Michigan's 2005 *Monitoring the Future* report, an annual survey of the behaviors and attitudes of secondary school students and college students, abuse of many illicit drugs, including ecstasy, methamphetamine, and marijuana, appears to be decreasing. At the same time, however, the recreational use of prescription pain-killers such as Vicodin and OxyContin is increasing, as is the nonmedical use of sedatives and sleeping pills. Another troubling finding indicates that inhalant abuse—the dangerous practice of sniffing paint thinner, glue, and other common household products—among eighth graders continues unabated.

Any discussion of the statistical prevalence of teen drug abuse and addiction, however, is complicated. Sociologist Mike Males, for instance, believes that the definition of teen addiction is hazy. He argues that the antidrug movement has defined abuse and addiction so broadly that it has blurred the line between drug use and serious, debilitating addiction. In a 2004 *Youth Today* article, Males urges society to question this trend—and the validity of reports and statistics that foster the perception that teen drug addiction is a serious problem:

> Crazed anti-youth panics are rampant. Institutional experts, popular authors, and media commentators eagerly recycle mythical scares over teenage heroin, Oxycontin, methamphetamine and cough-syrup epidemics—all despite scant credible evidence anything of the sort is occurring. When challenged (unfortunately, rarely), trumpeters of these fevered alarms marshal neither statistics nor real bodies to demonstrate their imagined hordes of grade-school junkies . . . exist in appreciable numbers. In truth, compared to their parents' Baby Boom generation, today's teenagers are better behaved in every measurable way. Data for today's teens show fewer violent deaths, drug overdoses, drunken driving, suicides, murders, births, abortions and serious crimes, and *more* graduations, college enrollment, community volunteerism and survey-reported self-confidence and optimism. . . . But reality means nothing. We're determined to believe kids today are horrifyingly dangerous and endangered.

Whether Males's assertion is correct or whether the problem is as serious as others report continues to be the focus of debate—one that is discussed in this anthology, *Contemporary Issues Companion: Teen Addiction*. The authors herein examine the breadth and scope of teen addiction, explore the factors that contribute to addiction, and debate what constitutes effective prevention and treatment. This volume also presents personal narratives of addiction and recovery. While the anthology looks at the problem of teen addiction from many angles, it cannot define the entire debate. Discussion on this subject will continue as parents, school and government officials, scientists, and others attempt to untangle the underlying causes of, and find solutions to, adolescent drug abuse and addiction.

CHAPTER 1

The Crisis of Teen Addiction

The Effects of Alcohol, Nicotine, and Other Drugs on the Adolescent Brain

David Walsh

In recent years, neuroscientists have discovered that the human brain undergoes massive structural changes during the teen years. According to David Walsh, tobacco, alcohol, and other drugs are particularly harmful when ingested during this intense developmental period. Much of the damage, Walsh writes, is due to the way that these drugs interact with the brain's neurotransmitters, the chemicals that regulate many body functions and affect mood, memory, learning, and perception. By interfering with these chemical messengers, Walsh contends, illicit drugs are particularly damaging to the adolescent brain, not only impairing memory and learning, but also contributing to addiction, depression, and other forms of psychological distress. David Walsh is a writer, psychologist, and the former executive director of the Fairview Treatment Program for Adolescents, the largest chemical dependency treatment center for adolescents in the United States.

I met hundreds of adolescents in the early '90s during my tenure as the executive director of the largest (and one of the best) chemical dependency treatment programs for adolescents in the country. Our program at Fairview University Medical Center in Minneapolis took the best of the adult recovery centers and tailored it to the unique problems of young addicts.

One of the patients, Lisa, seemed to have everything going for her. She was seventeen, smart, popular, pretty, but an alco-

David Walsh, from *Why Do They Act That Way?: A Survival Guide to the Adolescent Brain for You and Your Teen*. New York: Free Press, 2004, pp. 137–49. Copyright © 2004 by David Walsh, Ph.D. All rights reserved. Reprinted and edited with the permission of Free Press, a division of Simon & Schuster Adult Publishing Group. In the rest of the world by permission of the author, conveyed through Marly Rusoff Associates.

holic. Sad to say, Lisa's story—par for the course at Fairview—is widespread among teenagers today. In a recent study 30 percent of high school seniors qualified as heavy drinkers. Even more alarming, the same study showed that 14 percent of eighth graders fell into the same category. Unlike Lisa, many kids who get in over their heads with alcohol and drugs don't get the help they need. As alarming as her story may be, Lisa is one of the lucky ones.

When I met Lisa, she was a senior at an exclusive private high school in the Twin Cities. Her father was a prominent physician and her mother an active volunteer at the school Lisa and her sisters attended. Lisa told me she had had her first "real drink" when she was twelve and spending the night with a group of classmates at her friend Kathryn's house. Kathryn's parents had gone out for the evening "to give the girls some privacy." Before leaving, they told the girls the ground rules for their home. They also said they would be back by eleven o'clock. Within fifteen minutes of their departure Kathryn was opening a bottle of wine. She had taken it out of one of the boxes that her father had recently purchased at a big wine sale. "They bought cases of the stuff. They'll never miss it," she assured her wary friends. Kathryn's parents didn't miss it. They never knew. And so Lisa found something she liked a lot. Drinking on the sly was a bit of naughty mischief that made her feel grown-up. The adrenaline rush of the forbidden adventure and the good feeling she got from the wine made for a great combination. Best of all, getting away with it was so easy.

For the next five years Lisa's drinking continued—and increased. By the time she was fifteen, the weekend parties she attended routinely involved alcohol, pot, and occasionally some other drugs. Lisa tried everything that came her way, but her favorite was alcohol. She prided herself on the fact that she could hold her liquor as well as the guys. Sometimes she'd get into contests with the boys to see who could drink whom "under the table." Before long on nearly every Saturday morning she felt sick and had only a foggy memory of what had happened the night before.

Risky Behaviors

In addition to her drinking, Lisa made a habit of other risky activities, including unprotected oral sex. Like the alcohol use, her sexual activity became more and more frequent. Shortly before her sixteenth birthday, her boyfriend, Toby, talked her into sexual intercourse while she was drunk. After crossing that bridge she often combined drinking with sex with Toby. Eventually, having sex while drunk was something she did with other boys too.

After more than four years of alcohol use, Lisa's relationship with her parents began to deteriorate. The heated fights about curfews, declining grades, and blowing off chores escalated. If Lisa's parents suspected alcohol abuse, they never said anything about it to her, until the night came when Lisa's problem with alcohol was impossible to ignore. Luckily her parents were home when the call came from the hospital emergency room [ER]. Lisa's friends had taken her to the ER after she had passed out from heavy drinking. When her friends realized they couldn't wake her up, they hauled her unconscious body into a car and rushed her to the hospital. She was admitted with alcohol poisoning. Neither Lisa nor her friends could remember exactly how much she had had to drink that night, but the doctor said it had to have been a lot to get her blood alcohol level up to .40, five times the legal limit for intoxication in most states. When she did regain consciousness and was lucid enough to understand what he was saying, the ER doctor told Lisa how much danger she had been in. To put it simply, she was lucky to be alive.

Lisa's parents were shocked, but they were relieved that she had escaped death. Lisa promised them that she had learned her lesson. She also told them that this had been her first experience with drinking and that she would never do it again. Three months later the police caught Lisa and a group of her friends with an open liquor bottle in their car. Released without charges, she once again escaped relatively unscathed. And once again she promised her parents that she would steer clear of alcohol and any situations where it was present.

Helped Just in Time

Early in Lisa's senior year the assistant principal of her high school called her parents in for a conference. Lisa had been caught drinking on school grounds. The principal told Lisa's parents that teachers were hearing rumors that Lisa was drinking every day. He also told them that Lisa was suspended from school. He would not allow her to return until she had had a complete chemical dependency evaluation.

Lisa was referred to Fairview. The first several sessions of the evaluation didn't get very far. Lisa racked up hours of denial, inconsistent stories, and pleas to get off her back directed at her parents and the staff. But when Lisa walked into her last session with the evaluation team, she saw one of her best friends sitting in the room. The girl had tears streaming down her face. Lisa, taken aback by the presence of her friend, almost didn't notice her own parents and two sisters.

"What are you all doing here?" Lisa demanded.

"Lisa, I'm sorry. But I've agreed to tell your parents and the counselors everything," her friend said, in a shaky voice.

"Why don't you mind your own business?" Lisa said.

"Because I'm afraid you're going to end up pregnant, hurt, or dead!"

During the next hour the real story of Lisa's drinking finally started to come out. . . .

The Vulnerable Teen Brain

For years one argument against doing alcohol or drugs was based on a belief that everyone has a finite number of brain cells. No new brain cells would ever grow, no matter what. For the rest of your life, you could only maintain the number you had or lose them. Once they were gone, you weren't getting them back. Therefore scientists recommended that any activity that caused brain cell loss be avoided. Drinking and doing drugs, which kill large numbers of brain cells, are dangerous partly because, it was thought, they quickly depleted our finite supply. Doctors and counselors would typically say, "You shouldn't get drunk: it's just like hitting your head against the wall. You're killing parts of your brain that you'll never get back. Basically, you're just giving yourself brain damage."

According to research conducted by a team of neuroscientists in Sweden and the United States, it turns out that our brains can regenerate cells throughout the course of our lives. And . . . the number of brain cells you have isn't as important as how you fire and wire the ones you have. Even so, alcohol and drugs are probably even worse than we thought. Drugs and alcohol do more in the brain than simply kill brain cells.

By now practically everyone knows that a pregnant woman should not drink, smoke, or take any drugs not prescribed by her doctor. These prohibitions are not for the sake of the expectant mother; they're for the fetus inside her, which is particularly vulnerable to any foreign chemicals floating among the cells as they divide, multiply, and form organs and tissues. Alcohol and drugs can have a dramatically negative effect on fetal development. Fetal alcohol syndrome and "crack babies" provide tragic evidence that the brain and central nervous system are among the most vulnerable parts of the growing organism. There is no greater period of sensitivity than when the brain is growing during gestation. Foreign chemicals that work their way into the environment in which the brain is growing act like poison.

Prenatal and childhood development aren't the only important periods for the blossoming and pruning of neurons and their structures in the brain. The adolescent brain also has one of those intense developmental periods and is also very sensitive to foreign substances. In the following pages we shall see how recent research confirms that ingesting powerful chemicals like alcohol, tobacco, and other drugs during the adolescent "window of sensitivity" has very harmful effects.

Alcohol and the Adolescent Brain

Alcohol is the drug that is most likely to hurt an adolescent you know. Talk of cocaine, heroin, methamphetamine, and ecstasy strikes fear into the hearts of most parents, but the facts are clear that alcohol has been and continues to be the substance that does the most damage to the most kids. . . .

Most of the damage done by alcohol, tobacco, and other drugs during adolescence is due to their interference with neurotransmitters, the chemicals that transmit important messages across the synapses from neuron to neuron. Alcohol, nicotine, and other drugs inject chemicals into the brain, and these chemicals mix with the brain's chemical neurotransmitters, wreaking havoc on some important developmental processes.

For example, alcohol stimulates the release of dopamine, the feel-good neurotransmitter. That good feeling Lisa got when she drank was caused by alcohol-fueled surges of dopamine. Whenever you chronically use a foreign substance like alcohol to trigger dopamine surges, the body stops producing the levels of dopamine that it normally needs. As a result, you will feel worse and worse when you don't have alcohol in your system. Just at the time when your brain is trying to figure out how much of each chemical is needed—a crucial task of adolescence—alcohol gums up the works. Chronic drinkers like Lisa may feel great when they drink, but when they are sober and there's no alcohol-triggered dopamine, they feel awful.

Heavy alcohol use also interferes with the encoding of new memories. That's why it's hard to remember what happened after a night of heavy drinking. Alcohol's effect on short-term memory comes from its interference with a neurotransmitter called glutamate, which aids the neurons in storing new memories and in learning. When neurons fire together, glutamate helps them wire together and thus makes them more likely to fire together in the future. Without glutamate the neurons that fire together would not wire together. Alcohol makes it harder to learn and store new memories for anyone with a brain, young or old, but its effect on glutamate is *most* pronounced in the adolescent brain. Because adolescent brains are furiously blossoming, pruning, firing, and wiring, glutamate is even more crucial to adolescents than it is to people in other age groups. If glutamate effectiveness drops even a little bit, it can have a very negative effect on the sensitive adolescent brain. This teenage susceptibility to the negative effects of alcohol on glutamate functioning, and therefore on learning and memory, persists into the early twenties.

The results of alcohol use begin to add up. Research shows that heavy alcohol use can impair adolescent memory function by as much as 10 percent. Additional evidence shows that adolescents who are heavy drinkers have a smaller hippocampus, the brain structure that is key to the process of recording new memories, than nondrinkers. Thus *adolescents who drink a lot of alcohol end up having more memory and learning impairment than adults who drink the same amount,* because their brains are more susceptible to damage.

Alcohol's negative effect on learning and memory is bad news, but that's not the only problem. Adolescents are *over* sensitive to damage and *under* sensitive to the warning signs. For reasons that we do not yet understand, the sedation effects of alcohol are not as pronounced in the adolescent brain. The impairment of motor coordination is also delayed. That means that adolescents don't experience the two major warning signals that go off in the adult brain—sedation, or tiredness, and motor problems, like slurring words or stumbling—that indicate "I've had enough." It takes an adolescent drinker a lot more alcohol before sedation and motor coordination problems take effect. By then they can be dangerously drunk. In the absence of warning signals that tell them to stop, adolescent drinkers tend to drink more and do more damage to themselves. Adolescents like Lisa brag that they can "hold their liquor," but the fact that they're not showing outward signs of alcohol impairment doesn't mean they're *not* doing themselves serious damage. By the time the warning signals telling them to slow down show up, the physical harm of impaired reactions and memory damage has already occurred.

There's one more piece of bad news for adolescent drinkers. The earlier a youngster starts to drink, the higher the probability that he or she will have alcohol problems or alcoholism as an adult. This correlation probably occurs because drinking while the brain is developing encourages the brain to decide, through the firing and wiring process, that it needs alcohol. Adults would have to drink more heavily to be as likely to wire a tendency for alcohol use into their mature brains.

Tobacco

Tobacco contains chemicals that damage the adolescent brain. During the tobacco lawsuits in the mid-1990s tobacco companies were forced to turn over internal documents that revealed that they had deliberately targeted children and adolescents in their marketing and promotion efforts. They targeted the young because, although they may not have known brain science, they did know statistics. Research showed that if a young person got to the age of eighteen without lighting up, the odds were five to one that he or she would never use tobacco. Most habitual smokers began to use tobacco when they were adolescents. Big Tobacco targeted kids because they had to get them hooked by the time they graduated from high school or risk losing a lifelong customer.

A recent spate of adolescent tobacco use studies has shown that nicotine, like alcohol, affects the adolescent brain differently than it affects an adult's. Adolescents are much more likely than adults to get addicted to nicotine, the most prominent and powerful chemical in tobacco, and they get addicted much more quickly.

Nicotine's potent effect on the brain is due to its influence on almost two dozen neurotransmitters. Nicotine quickly increases the number of receptors (docking stations) for itself in some key brain areas so that the brain quickly adapts to the presence of nicotine and reacts negatively when it is absent. Each time a person smokes, in other words, his brain will extend its desire for more nicotine. And when he is not smoking, he will crave the drug and have physical symptoms of withdrawal that make quitting cold turkey very difficult.

At the same time that nicotine makes a home for itself in the brain, it behaves again like alcohol by increasing the production of dopamine. Smokers really do feel good when they have a cigarette, because their dopamine levels rise. And because their bodies depend on nicotine for that dopamine surge, they begin to feel lousy if they go a long time without a cigarette.

Nicotine has a triple whammy on adolescents which makes it extremely addictive: it increases dopamine; it increases the number of nicotine receptors in the neurons; and it affects the mix of neurotransmitters. This triumvirate of trouble makes it especially hard for adolescents to quit.

To make matters worse, adolescents are more likely than adults to use tobacco as a springboard to using other, more powerful drugs. Tobacco is truly a gateway drug: smoking makes it easier for adolescents to try other drugs. Research shows that kids who smoke are at higher risk for using alcohol and other substances.

Of course there are a lot of health reasons to be concerned about tobacco too. The link between nicotine and a host of diseases, including certain types of cancer, heart disease, lung disease, and overall susceptibility to disease, is undeniable.

More than 400,000 people die of tobacco-related illnesses every year in the United States. It's a shame then that 3,000 kids start on this deadly addiction every day. . . .

Other Drugs

Alcohol and nicotine are two big, real problems for teens, but most parents are more concerned that their kids will get into other, "harder" drugs. Even though we shouldn't forget how serious alcohol and nicotine are, we have reason to be concerned about other drugs as well. The common thread among all these drugs is their effects on neurotransmitters, especially increasing the levels of dopamine. Each drug has its own unique chemical interaction, but dopamine figures into every picture.

Kids get very mixed messages about marijuana. Many parents today grew up during the sixties, seventies, and eighties using marijuana themselves. It didn't seem to hurt them much, if at all, at the time they used it, and adults who used the drug back then for the most part do not notice any lingering effects. But what adults and parents need to remember is that marijuana today has 500 percent more THC, the active ingredient in marijuana, than the pot they smoked. THC increases levels of dopamine and can affect adversely how the brain makes its own dopamine. This means that today's teens who smoke pot are more likely to become addicted to it and to suffer the side effects of short-term memory loss, problems with concentration, and lack of coordination that have always been associated with marijuana. These problems are in addition to those that frequent users have with loss of motivation.

Cocaine is physically and psychologically dangerous because it affects three neurotransmitters. It interferes with the reabsorption of dopamine, causing the levels of the neurotransmitter to keep increasing, which leads to a state of euphoria. Cocaine also increases serotonin, which can lead to an inflated sense of confidence and to higher levels of another neurotransmitter, norepinephrine, resulting in greater energy. Together these three neurotransmitters contribute to the infamous cocaine high.

Ecstasy is especially dangerous because brain studies have shown that it interferes with the normal transport of serotonin, an effect that can permanently damage learning and memory. There has been mention in the popular press that ecstasy causes "holes in the brain." While not true in a literal sense, this metaphor refers to evidence of long-term damage to the cells that release serotonin. In addition reports have shown that some people who use ecstasy heavily as adolescents go on to have chronic, severe problems with depression in their adult lives.

A recent trend in drug abuse among younger adolescents is the use of nonprescription cough and cold medicines that are easily available in supermarkets and drugstores everywhere. Most of these remedies contain dextromethorphan or DXM, a cough suppressant that can produce hallucinations in high doses. Websites tell kids how much medicine they need to get high, depending on their weight. "Robotripping" or "dexing" requires less than a bottle and only costs a few dollars. Overdosing is on the rise, with some emergency rooms reporting as many as four cases a week among adolescents as young as twelve. Five young teens died of overdoses between 2002 and 2003. Symptoms of abuse include sweating, fever, dry skin, blurred vision, hallucinations, nausea, irregular heartbeat, and loss of consciousness.

Because of the adolescent brain's window of sensitivity while important neural circuits are being formed, the negative effect of alcohol, nicotine, and other drugs on the adolescent brain is faster and more severe and occurs with less warning than in the adult brain. The negative effects of these chemicals aren't just temporary altered states of mind or behavior problems: they can damage a developing brain permanently. Drugs and alcohol can be a serious problem for anyone, but for adolescents they can become a serious problem forever.

The Teen Drug Crisis Is Exaggerated

Mike Males, interviewed by Drug War Chronicle

In an interview with the Drug War Chronicle, *a publication of the national drug policy reform organization Drug Reform Coordination Network (DRCNet), sociologist Mike Males argues that "America is in a punishing, terrified rage against youth." This hostility toward young people, Males states, results in a misguided tendency to disproportionately blame America's youth for society's ills—drug addiction, AIDS, and crime, for example. In reality, the teen drug crisis does not exist, nor is the problem even remotely similar to that claimed by the government's war on drugs. Today's teens, Males concludes, are far less drug-addicted than their parents and other adults of the primarily white, middle-aged, baby boom generation—indeed, the fastest growing population in terms of drug abuse. Mike Males is a professor at the University of California at Santa Cruz and has written extensively on youth issues, including such books as* The Scapegoat Generation: America's War on Adolescents *and* Framing Youth: Ten Myths About the Next Generation.

Drug War Chronicle: *You have written extensively about the scapegoating of youth. Generally, what do you mean by that? How is it manifested?*

Professor Mike Males: Thirty years ago, [anthropologist] Margaret Mead wrote that adults in societies experiencing rapid social change automatically fear youths as symbols of an alien, menacing future [that] older age groups don't comprehend. While most cultures have taken steps to keep generations connected, Americans—experiencing not just social, but racial

Mike Males, interviewed by *Drug War Chronicle*, "Youth Sociologist Mike Males," November 21, 2003. http://Stopthedrugwar.org. Reproduced by permission.

evolution—have let fear and hostility toward youth rage out of control. Today's American adults are irrationally afraid of youths and imagine that young people—particularly in cities and states in which aging adults are white and youths are increasingly non-white—harbor unheard-of dangers and threats. Private industries have arisen to profit from grownup fright toward the young and advance their interests by inflaming them further. As a result, virtually every American social problem today—drugs, drinking, smoking, violence, crime, guns, imprisonment, AIDS, obesity, poverty, anti-social behavior, bad moral values—are quickly converted into epidemics caused by youths. Private and political interests across the spectrum push their own solutions to punish, manage and redirect the supposedly out-of-control young.

In reality, however, every standard measure shows that it is not teenagers but aging baby boomers who are causing today's most serious, fastest-growing problems with drug addiction, crime, imprisonment, AIDS, and family and community disarray. Because the older generation refuses to face its problems, it inflicts especially vicious stigmas and disinvestments on younger generations. As a result of rising adult paranoia that has no basis in reality, America is in a punishing, terrified rage against youths—one, unfortunately, fed by interests from left to right across the spectrum. I spent a lot of time in *Scapegoat Generation* (1996) and *Framing Youth* (1999) showing that nearly all the imagined youth crises of today—from guns to heroin to suicide—are hallucinations. They simply do not exist, and the big problems are among the middle-agers. It is a disgraceful situation, and both the war on drugs and its reformist opponents advance their goals by deploying the worst disinformation about youth while ignoring the crisis of addiction, crime, and rigidly punishing moralism among older Americans that threaten young people far more than drugs ever did.

Drug Abuse Among Adults

America's most catastrophic social crisis over the last 25 years has been the explosion in hard-drug abuse among aging baby boomers. More than 100,000 Americans over age 30 have died from overdoses of illegal drugs since 1980, and untold thousands more have died from illicit-drug effects, such as accidents and chronic abuse, and millions have been hospitalized in drug emergencies. Today the fastest growing population in terms of drug abuse, criminal arrest for violent, property, and drug offenses, and imprisonment is persons aged 35 to 59, mostly white. This middle-aged crisis underlies a parallel explosion in felony crime and imprisonment, family violence and community disruption, and drug-supply gangs whose conflicts have contributed to the murders of thousands of inner-city young men at the street level of drug distribution. The most recent federal Drug Abuse Warning Network figures, for 2001 and 2002, show drug abuse deaths and hospital emergencies are at record levels, worse than at any time in known history.

Yet no one—certainly not the drug war, and bafflingly not reformers—mentions this middle-aged drug crisis, which has skyrocketed every year as the drug war has escalated. Instead, drug reform groups have tamely gone along with the drug war's hysterical obsession with whether a few teens smoke pot, which is a non-issue. Teens comprise perhaps 2% of America's drug problem, but 90% of the raging controversy over drug use. That is scapegoating.

The Crisis Does Not Exist

Chronicle: *How does the war on drugs play into targeting young people?*

Males: The drug war has prospered—despite its massive failure to stem drug abuse after spending hundreds of billions of dollars and arresting 13 million people over the past 20 years—by constantly whipping up fears of adolescents. Nearly every ONDCP [Office of National Drug Control Policy], Partnership for a Drug-Free America, and CASA [The National Center on Addiction and Substance Abuse at Columbia University] press release today claims a massive, conveniently hidden teenage drug crisis—the crisis rotates from coke to pot to heroin to meth to ecstasy to Oxycontin, etc.—terrible scourges they claim parents would be terrified of if they knew about them.

The teen drug crisis does not exist. I've investigated nearly every one of them. There is no evidence of teenage deaths, hospital ER [emergency room] cases, or even addiction-related crime by youths that would be obvious if any real youth drug abuse epidemic existed. Rather, it is fear of some imagined youth crisis that drives the war on drugs. [The] *San Francisco Chronicle* reports [that ONDCP director] John Walters was in San Francisco campaigning against medical marijuana because he says it makes pot sound harmless, leading many youths to smoke it when many are supposedly in treatment for pot abuse. Another article says an Oakland youth center has to move because medical marijuana clubs in "Oaksterdam"[1] are a bad influence on kids. And on and on. It's easy to refute Walters' hysteria; the vast majority of youths forced into treatment for pot are there not for dependency, but for "non-dependent abuse," which mainly means just "use."

But the larger point is Walters' and drug warriors' relentless campaign to tie marijuana and other drugs to teenagers. Why do they do this? We spend a lot of time refuting wild exaggerations of the health dangers of pot or ecstasy, which is fine. But what we have to recognize is that a drug isn't illegal because of its potential for damage—or else hard liquor and tobacco would be outlawed—but because of who is perceived as using the drug. Teenagers are an unpopular, feared, even

1. This term is meant to express that there are so many state-legal medical marijuana shops in Oakland that the city can be compared to the city of Amsterdam in Holland where pot is legally available in coffee shops.

hated minority in the US that is falsely depicted as causing terrible social problems. In fact, teens use pot as responsibly as adults do, and they aren't causing terrible problems—but the fearsome image created by the drug war is one of a massive, frightening youth crisis.

Scare Tactics and False Claims

Unfortunately, several drug policy reform groups have issued public statements reinforcing the drug war's distorted claim that teens are suffering some kind of drug abuse crisis and agreeing that stopping teens from using any drug should be our drug policy's overriding goal. This is not simply dishonest, it's a politically insane strategy for reformers to pursue. What they are saying is that marijuana is so dangerous to teens that we should marshal the drug war to enforce absolute teen prohibition. Bizarrely, they somehow think this tactic will build support for their nonsensical claim that legalizing marijuana for adults will stop teens from getting it.

These groups comb dozens of surveys (including ones such as CASA's and PRIDE's [Parents' Resource Institute for Drug Education] that are completely biased and unreliable) that measure use of dozens of drugs across multiple adolescent groups and drug-use categories such as lifetime, monthly, etc.—hundreds of numbers each year, which always show some drugs are being used a bit more and some a bit less—in order to selectively ferret out any increase in teen use, no matter how insignificant. They then issue alarmist press releases alleging huge increases in this or that category of teenage coke or heroin or pot use and blaming the drug war for failing to "protect our children." Those kind of emotional, prohibitionist scare tactics are exactly what we condemn drug warriors for exploiting.

Meanwhile, 200 separate surveys by more reliable entities such as Monitoring the Future and the National Household Survey show without exception that teens find legal drugs such as alcohol and tobacco far easier to get, and use them far more, than illegal drugs. The best information is that if we legalize marijuana, a few more teens and adults will use it, and that is no cause for panic. Surveys clearly show strong correlations between adult drinking, smoking, and marijuana use—where adults use a lot, so do teens.

Crazier still, a few reform lobbies have even supported plans to continue arresting, even imprisoning, persons under 21 for even the smallest marijuana infraction as a ploy to win greater support for legalizing marijuana for use by adults. That is not reform; it just reinforces the drug war's traditional repressions aimed at younger, feared groups. Other, more responsible drug reform groups issue meaningless statements that pretend we can devise some "realistic" anti-drug education scheme aimed at teens that will lead to a society in which adults can party but teens will abstain. It can't be done and shouldn't be tried because it represents a fundamentally misplaced priority.

Youths have already demonstrated that they know the difference between hard and soft drugs. The vast majority of teen drug use today consists of (a) beer, (b) social, that is, weekend or occasional, cigarette smoking, (c) marijuana, and (d) ecstasy. They use softer drugs in more moderate quantities than adults do. That is why so few teens are dying from drugs or getting addicted. It is a major irony that today's adolescents already follow the very model of "harm reduction" that drug reform groups want to see society as a whole adopt, and yet we insist on depicting the teens as in some kind of terrible danger.

Rethinking Drug Reform

Trying to scare the public about teens is not just useless. The whole scheme of focusing on teenage drug use is just plain crazy for drug reformers. This country will never legalize pot as long as it remains so frightened of its youth and ready to believe any terrible thing any self-interest group says. In fact, teenage drug use is the least of our problems. We need to turn down the heat on this issue. Drug reform groups need to go back to basic honesty—drug abuse (not use) is the problem, older (not younger) groups are suffering from addiction crises, the drug war's diversionary distortions about teens and its punitive policies have only made these worse, and it's time to spell out why America is caught up in its worst drug abuse crisis in history right now—record peaks in hospitalizations and deaths from illegal drugs, as well as drug-related imprisonments, in 2001 and 2002. The worst crisis is a very real, gigantic increase in drug abuse by hundreds of thousands of older-agers—mostly white folks—that no one will talk about precisely because our real drug abusers are higher status, mainstream populations.

The Netherlands has done many fine things with drug policy, and its first step to reform was to change the public image of who abuses drugs from relatively harmless use of soft drugs by young people to the reality of hard-drug abuse by aging addicts. Unfortunately, the Dutch do a terrible job of surveys. You can find a Dutch survey to document anything you want about drug use. The only long-term ones, by the Trimbos Institute, indicate marijuana use was rare among Dutch teens 20 years ago but has since risen to levels comparable with the US. Clearly, the Dutch don't care much about whether 5% or 10% of their teens smoke pot in a given month, and we shouldn't either. It's irrelevant. The real victory is that the Netherlands brought down its heroin death rate by 50% over the past 20 years while heroin deaths in the US quadrupled.

Scapegoating Youth

Chronicle: *Are you saying that teen drug use is less than it's cracked up to be?*

Males: Teen drug use goes up and down, but teen drug abuse (in terms of overdose deaths) is far rarer today than it was 30 years ago, and far lower than middle-aged drug abuse today. Drug reform groups should stop trying to exploit fear of teenagers and just state the facts: Teens are not the drug problem, teenage use of marijuana is not a serious issue, and teens are far more endangered by the drug war's dereliction in preventing manifest drug abuse among their parents and other adults than they are by their own adolescent drug experimentation. Meredith Maran's new book, *Dirty*, is fine when it sticks to profiles of individual teen drug abusers, but it is a disaster when it claims a massive teenage drug epidemic and evades the far worse drug abuse in her own baby boom generation.

Chronicle: *What should be done about teen drug use?*

Males: Let them handle it—we have no choice in any case. We should have confidence in teens' judgment and learn from them. Teens are using milder drugs (beer, marijuana, ecstasy) in safer settings than adults, which is why teens suffer so few overdoses and deaths today. Of 20,000 drug overdose deaths in 2000, just 475 were under age 20—16,000 were over age 30. Leave teens alone. Look instead at drug abuse by their parents, whose bad example of heroin, cocaine, meth, mixed-drug, and alcohol combined with drug abuse is the best (and most painful) education of the younger generation against hard drug abuse ever.

Chronicle: *You talk about teens being scapegoated, but what about the issue of teen safety being used as a wedge for restricting the freedom of adults? And are reformers falling into this trap?*

Males: Exactly—hysteria that a teen [drug-use crisis] might blaze up if pot were legalized is the central fear the drug war exploits to keep pot illegal. It's a phony fear—neither criminalization nor legalization has anything to do with teen pot use. The Netherlands decriminalized pot and allowed its sale in coffee shops, and Dutch teenage marijuana use tripled during the 1980s and 1990s. The US arrested millions of people (half under age 21) for marijuana use in the 1980s and 1990s, and teenage marijuana use rose rapidly here as well. As of today, it's a wash—Dutch teens are no more likely to use marijuana than US teens. Both drug warriors and drug reformers have lied shamelessly about whether Dutch-style legalization or US-style punitive prohibition better deters teens from smoking pot. In fact, neither approach has any relevance. Teens smoke pot in accordance with the adult customs of their respective countries, and the legal regime makes no difference.

Interestingly, surveys indicate that in years in which US teen pot-smoking is more prevalent, such as the late 1970s and mid-1990s, teenage death rates from drug overdoses of all kinds (already very low) go lower still. When fewer teens use pot, harder drug fatalities rise. It is time to get the calamitous, 125-year US drug war off dead center. Exploiting fear of drug use by unpopular, feared populations—whether Chinese and opium, blacks and cocaine, Mexicans and marijuana, or teens and any drug—just feeds the irrational panic that drives the drug war. America's drug abuse crisis is mainstream middle-American, middle-aged, and white. We should say that directly.

The Teen Drug Crisis
Is Escalating

Meredith Maran

*America is in the grip of a teen drug abuse crisis, reports jour-
nalist and author Meredith Maran. In Maran's view, the epidemic of teen drug use exploded across the nation during the
1960s and has progressed relatively unchecked, despite well-
intentioned but ultimately futile attempts by schools and other
institutions to contain the problem. To Maran, this crisis mirrors
society at large—that is, a widespread drug crisis that affects
Americans of all ages and backgrounds. Meredith Maran is the
author of* Dirty: A Search for Answers Inside America's Teenage Drug Epidemic, *from which the following is excerpted.*

I've been writing books and articles about teenagers since I
was one myself, driven then as now by the same Big Question—the question that drove me to smoke my first joint and
write my first book in high school, the question that drives
me still: How and why are things in America so different from
the way they're supposed to be?

This question opens another one. What can the lives of
teenagers—no longer cosseted as children, but not yet accountable as adults—teach us about the price of our broken
promises?

I know the price. I've paid it, first as a raging teenager,
then as the mother of one. . . . What had I done or failed to
do for my younger son, Jesse, that led him to spend his teenage years high on pot and alcohol, running the streets, in jail?

Jesse's first arrest was for shoplifting at age thirteen; his
last was a DUI [driving under the influence] at age twenty.

During the years in between, the only thing I could count on was the steady escalation of his arrests and school suspensions—from fighting on campus to joyriding; from stealing checkbooks and wallets to stealing bicycles; and finally, to breaking a bottle over a kid's head, sending him to the hospital. I lived through those years in a protracted state of shock: mid-traumatic stress I can still summon now just by writing about it. Sleepless nights blurred into bad-news days; brief interludes of "normal life" were shattered by phone calls summoning me and my ex-husband to principals' offices, police stations, emergency rooms, jails.

Who or What Is to Blame?

What, I asked myself and everyone else, did my suffering child need? Why couldn't I, or his devoted dad, or the many trained professionals we enlisted give it to him? Why was Jesse's one-year-older brother, Peter, gliding through adolescence—smoking plenty of pot, blowing off plenty of homework, but doing just fine in school, at home, in life—while Jesse rarely went a day without getting high, a week without a heart-stopping drama? From birth Jesse had been exceptional: brilliant, artistic, complex. Alternately horrifying and astounding his teachers with his precocious cartooning, satiric story writing, and razor-tongued wit, he was suspended from preschool for biting, from fourth grade for disrupting class, from junior high for threatening the dean. By the time Jesse got to high school, he didn't seem so exceptional anymore. He seemed like any other wanna-be thug.

At age twenty, after his final stint in jail, Jesse started going to church. He stopped drinking and smoking pot. He stopped committing crimes. Today, at twenty-three, Jesse lives a life of service to others. My son the teenage felon works, now, at a residential treatment program for drug-addicted teenagers. My son the (ethnic, if not religious) Jew is now the youngest and the only white minister at a predominantly African American Baptist church. He credits God with saving his soul, and his life.

I blamed myself for Jesse's problems, of course, just as I'd spent twenty years in therapy blaming my mother for mine. But as this admirable young man emerged from the tempest of his adolescence, I began to wonder where else the responsibility might lie. What did Jesse's struggle *mean* in the bigger picture of our nation's epidemic of teenagers in crisis?

The mistakes I'd made with Jesse were legion, but they couldn't explain why my home state of California, among others, was building more jails than schools; why business was booming nationwide for wilderness programs, therapeutic boarding schools, and adolescent rehab centers. Nor could my failings explain my friends' problems with *their* kids. My friends, I knew, were attentive, smart, loving parents—rich, middle-class, and poor; black, white, and brown; gay, straight, and other, raising their kids in all kinds of styles and cultures. Yet their teenagers were having trouble too, suffering in any of the myriad ways that teenagers in America suffer and manifest their suffering.

I'd talked my friend Stephen through hiring professional kidnappers to "escort" his heroin-addicted daughter to a therapeutic boarding school in the middle of the night. I'd told my friend Valerie to search her son's sock drawer, then comforted her when she found pot and bullets in an incense box there. I'd advised my friend Chris about what she could and could not bring inside when she went to visit her alcoholic daughter in Juvenile Hall. I'd mediated in the verging-on-violent screaming matches between my *comadre* María, the finest parent and the finest woman I knew, and her stoned and raging teenage son.

Psychological Wounds

I knew that, like Jesse, my friends' kids had issues beyond drug abuse: psychological and social wounds deeper than the needle tracks on their arms. Where, I wondered, did those wounds come from? How can we—as families, communities, a nation—treat or, better yet, prevent them? And why are so many of our children in so much pain in the first place?

I've long believed that teenagers are the canary in America's mine: old enough to know what's wrong around them, young enough to name and condemn it unreservedly. Their alienation and their anger mirror and exacerbate our own. As William Finnegan says in the final words of his 1998 classic, *Cold New World*, "What young people show us is simply the world we have made for them."

What does our children's drug use show us—about them, about us, about the world we've made for them? By asking the Big Questions about teenage drug use, I went looking for Big Answers. I went looking for what I needed, a few short years ago, to help ease my son's anguish and my own.

This is what I found.

More Teenagers than Ever Are Using Drugs

America's drug crisis is a runaway train. Keeping teenagers from jumping on board—or being flattened on the tracks—is the linchpin of the nation's efforts to stop it. Research shows that if you don't use drugs as a kid, you're less likely to use drugs as an adult. Keeping teens clean today, the logic goes, equals fewer adult addicts tomorrow. The strategy is a reasonable one. The problem is, it hasn't worked.

Despite countless attempts by governments, schools, churches, and families to contain the epidemic of teen drug use that exploded across the nation during the 1960s, the epidemic has been escalating (with an occasional downward blip) ever since. Thirty years into the government's multi-billion-dollar campaign to steer kids away from drugs and fifteen years since we were all mesmerized by that single egg frying in the pan—"This is your brain. This is your brain on drugs"

—in turn-of-the-millennium America more teenagers are using drugs than ever in the history of this country, or any country in the world.

One-fourth of the high-school seniors in America today have problems with drugs and alcohol. Nearly two-thirds of the teenagers in America today do drugs before they finish high school—one-third of them by the time they're in eighth grade. (Do the math: we're talking twelve-year-olds.) Fifty-six percent of seventeen-year-olds know at least one drug dealer at school.

Nothing we're doing about it is working. Not the ads, not the DARE programs in the schools, not the after-school specials on TV. Not the glitzy rehab spas, the grimy public treatment centers, the fancy boarding schools. Not the Juvenile Halls, the youth detention camps, the jails.

By the time they're seniors in high school:

50 percent of teenagers have binged on alcohol (chugged five or more drinks in a row).

41 percent have smoked pot.

12.5 percent have taken tranquilizers or barbiturates.

12 percent have taken Ecstasy ("X" use was up 71 percent between 1999 and 2001).

11 percent have used amphetamines ("speed" in its various forms).

10 percent have taken LSD.

9 percent have used cocaine, about half in the form of crack.

9 percent have sniffed inhalants.

4 percent have snorted or shot heroin.

Two hundred thousand American teenagers were arrested for drug violations in 1999, an increase of 291 percent over the past decade. Seven out of ten juveniles who get in trouble with the law test positive for drugs. Nine out of ten teenagers who need drug treatment aren't getting it.

These are your kids. These are your kids on drugs.

We Are All Paying for Drug Use

Welcome to America, where on any given day, one million people are in treatment for drug or alcohol abuse. The number one health problem in the nation, substance abuse causes more death and illness than any other preventable condition. Four times as many women die from addiction-related illness, for example, as die from breast cancer.

Nearly fifteen million Americans—6.3 percent of the population age twelve and over—are illicit-drug users. Half of them are under age twenty-six. All told, they spend $60 billion a year on the illegal stuff they smoke, snort, swallow, and shoot.

Whether you indulge or not, you're paying for the party. Drug abuse costs the U.S. economy $414 billion a year. Besides the health and productivity costs, President [George W.] Bush's War on Drugs swallows $19.2 billion. Two-thirds of that is spent on law enforcement and interdiction (kicking in housing-project doors, making sure the people who get busted go to jail). With no apparent comprehension of cause and effect—only 3.6 percent of the War on Drugs budget is allotted for treatment, 2.4 percent for prevention—the Bush administration acknowledges that most people who need treatment aren't getting it.

More than one million people a year are arrested for drugs, contributing generously to one of our nation's most dubious achievements: the United States has the second-highest—and the fastest-growing—incarceration rate in the world. Sixty percent of the nearly two million people in our prisons today are drug offenders. If the prison population keeps increasing at its current rate (6.6 million Americans—one in every thirty-two adults—are currently incarcerated, on probation, or on parole), by 2053 there will be more Americans in jail than out.

This is your country. This is your country on drugs.

Methamphetamine Is Today's Teen Drug of Choice

Michael J. Weiss

Methamphetamine—also known as ice, crank, or crystal—is a cheap and widely available drug that is becoming increasingly prevalent in rural, suburban, and urban communities alike. According to Michael J. Weiss, methamphetamine has evolved into the drug of choice for many adolescents who do not fit the stereotype of teens who typically use illicit drugs. Indeed, methamphetamine tends to be popular among seemingly well-adjusted teens who excel in academics and participate in a variety of extracurricular activities. Because methamphetamine is a powerful stimulant that can profoundly heighten a user's energy, it may particularly appeal to young people struggling to meet the demands of a rigorous schedule. Weiss warns, however, that methamphetamine is highly addictive, and the road to recovery may be long and painful, if not impossible, to traverse. Michael J. Weiss is a journalist, author, and contributing editor to Ladies' Home Journal, *in which the following article originally appeared.*

Katy Knutson was the last person that neighbors in her upscale Minneapolis suburb expected to become a drug addict. The petite high school junior was an honors student, a member of the varsity swim team, and a regular churchgoer. But when a friend turned her on to methamphetamine in late 2003, she quickly succumbed to the drug's viselike grip. "It made me feel like the most beautiful and powerful person in the world," says Katy, now 18. "My concentration at school shot up. I felt like I could walk through walls."

For two months, Katy went on a binge, snorting several lines of meth powder a day. The initial euphoric rush was invariably followed by a harrowing crash that left her irritable, depressed, and paranoid. After getting high she would stay awake nights, then sleep for hours, straight through meals (dropping from 115 to 92 pounds in the process). She began skipping school, avoiding church, and stealing money from her parents' wallets to buy more meth. As Katy's sweet personality turned caustic, her desperate parents, who'd learned she was hooked after a few weeks, tried to break the drug's hold. "We yelled, we bribed her with new clothes, we sent her to Alcoholics Anonymous," says Katy's mother, Moira Knutson, 47, a high-school aide. "Nothing worked."

Katy hit bottom on a frigid night in December 2003 when police found her wandering the streets in a light jacket, high and disoriented. The next day, her parents sent her to an out-of-town treatment facility, then to a group home for teenage girls—three and a half months in all. Knutson and her husband, an administrator at a law firm, agonized over their decision. But Katy's addiction had pushed them to a breaking point. "We worried that she could die from meth," recalls Moira.

For Katy, kicking meth was as difficult as getting hooked had been easy. She endured body-racking tremors and endless insomnia. "I wanted one last hit to feel better," she recalls. Finally, after months of therapy, Katy moved back in with her parents, clear-eyed and drug-free. She recently graduated from Sobriety High, a school for student addicts in Edina, Minnesota, and will enroll next month at the College of St. Catherine, in St. Paul. She still attends a recovery program three nights a week to fortify her resolve. "It's a hard drug to let go of," Katy says. "But I feel like I've finally turned the corner." Those traumatic months, she says, "were hell—for me and everyone around me."

Drug Siege in the Suburbs

The anguish experienced by the Knutsons is being played out all over the country in what has quietly become a suburban youth drug epidemic. Also known as "crystal," "ice," or "crank," methamphetamine is a powerful, highly addictive stimulant that is widely available in pills or powder form; the latter can be snorted, smoked, swallowed, or injected. Cheaply sold on the street for as little as $5 a hit, it's also therefore affordable for most teens. Originally popular among California biker gangs in the 1980s, meth has made its way east, infecting rural, suburban, and urban communities alike. While there are no nationwide statistics on meth use strictly among teens, a 2004 federal government survey found that 6.2 percent of 12th graders have used meth—a figure that experts say is vastly underreported.

What makes meth so dangerous is its addictiveness: It can be virtually impossible for someone to try it just once. "With meth, there's no such thing as a casual user," says Joseph Frascella, PhD, a neuroscientist at the National Institute on Drug Abuse, in Bethesda, Maryland. "The younger someone starts using meth, the worse the outcome." And because it can be easier to get hold of than beer or cigarettes, meth is often becoming the first drug that teenagers use. Because meth stimulates the central nervous system and causes the brain to release pleasure-inducing dopamine, it leaves kids feeling euphoric, brilliant, and in control—qualities normally in scarce supply during adolescence. And the high from a single dose can last 14 hours.

Over time and with ever-larger doses (as with most addictive drugs, a habitual user needs bigger doses to get the same high) these effects deteriorate into less-desirable ones: irritability, insomnia, anxiety, aggressiveness, tremors, and paranoia. With prolonged use, meth disrupts neurotransmitters in the brain, slowing cognitive and motor functions. "It's a powerful stimulant that blasts the brain. To put it bluntly, it makes you slower and stupider over time," says Dr. Frascella. Researchers do not yet know whether these effects are permanent. But they do know that sustained, high doses can cause a rise in heart rate, resulting in strokes and convulsions that can be fatal. Experts also say that geographic areas with high meth use have a greater incidence of psychotic episodes among teenagers, which, in rare cases, may have led to suicide.

The Best and Brightest Teens

Teens who decide to try meth don't fit the stereotype of kids who get stoned and retreat to their rec room to zone out in front of the TV. Meth often appeals to outstanding students who want an energy boost to cope with heavy academic and extracurricular loads. Among teenage girls, meth's ability to suppress appetite makes it especially popular. A 2004 study of 305 teenagers by Richard Rawson, PhD, associate director of integrated substance abuse programs at UCLA, found that girls are three times more likely than boys to choose meth over marijuana and alcohol. In fact, among some suburban teens, meth is known as "the Jenny Crank diet."

Alexander Smith [a pseudonym], a 17-year-old honors student from suburban Nashville, watched his weight drop from 150 to 118 pounds during his four-month binge in early 2004. He liked the extra stamina meth gave him, which helped him keep up with advanced-placement classes and his after-school lawn-mowing business. "It gave me more energy than my body could handle," he recalls. Soon he was smoking not just for the buzz, but to avoid the hangover that followed the high. He kept taking meth even as his heart rate climbed to 180 beats per minute—almost three times the normal rate—and he experienced hallucinations and suicidal thoughts.

Meanwhile, his parents seemed oblivious to his secret life. Smith's mother, 42, an elementary school nurse, admits that she and her salesman husband were fooled. Smith continued to get good grades. When he'd sleep all afternoon, she chalked it up to typical teenage sloth. "We realized what was going on only when the police called at 1 a.m. on a school night to tell us our son had been arrested for possessing and intending to sell drugs," she says. "We thought he was in bed asleep." [In] April [2005] Smith was arrested again, this time for selling the attention deficit disorder prescription drug Adderall at school, and then a third time for failing a drug test before his trial. Convictions on all three counts earned him nine days in jail, six months on probation, and expulsion from school. He has since entered a treatment program and now attends Community High School for recovering addicts in Nashville.

Such naivete is all too common. A 2004 study of 1,205 parents by the nonprofit group Partnership for a Drug-Free America found that only 1 percent of parents believed their teens had ever used synthetic drugs. "These chemical drugs are much more powerful than the marijuana and cocaine baby-boomer parents used as teens," says Partnership president Steve Pasierb. "Most parents are clueless that meth is one of the most dangerous drugs out there."

Drug Pushers Next Door

How has meth so effectively infiltrated the suburbs? Its active ingredients are legal (pseudoephedrine is found in common over-the-counter cold remedies). "And it's made from a recipe that any chemistry student can follow," says Karen Tandy, a spokesperson for the Drug Enforcement Administration in Arlington, Virginia. While much of the country's meth supply is made in so-called super labs in Mexico and Southern California run by organized crime and street gangs, one-third is produced in "mom-and-pop" meth labs in hotel rooms, homes, garages, even in the trunks of cars. A mere $200 can buy the ingredients to produce an ounce of meth (enough to get 100 people high), and "cooking" instructions can be downloaded from the Internet. (A Google search for "meth recipe" turned up some 30,000 hits.) "Everything you need can be bought at drug and hardware stores," says Shannon Brant, 34, a meth addict who used to supply pseudoephedrine to a meth manufacturer outside Atlanta. Brant would enlist the help of girlfriends to buy 100 boxes of medicine at a time. "We'd go into one place and each buy three packs of cold pills, then do the same at other stores," she recalls. When Brant had accumulated enough pills, she'd take them to a lab, where she'd receive some of the finished product as payment.

The labs have bred a crime wave of burglaries, thefts, and even murder in surrounding communities. But a crackdown is under way. More than 17,000 meth labs and dump sites nationwide were shut down [in 2004], according to the federal Office of National Drug Control Policy, in Washington, D.C. More than 20 states have enacted sales restrictions [since 2003] on pseudoephedrine in common cold remedies and other meth precursor products. The first major bill, passed [in] April [2005] in Oklahoma, classifies decongestants in tablet form as controlled substances and bans their sale in convenience and grocery stores. It also requires that pharmacies put these remedies behind locked counters, limit the quantities sold per customer, and require buyers to show a photo ID and sign a logbook. Since the law went into effect, busts of illegal meth labs across the state have dropped from roughly 100 to 25 a month. Experts feared the law would simply drive meth makers into other states—an outcome that has prompted legislators elsewhere to adopt their own regulations in defense. [As of August 2005], seven states had passed laws similar to Oklahoma's, and 30 more were considering doing so.

[In] January [2005], Senators Dianne Feinstein and Jim Talent, of California and Missouri, respectively, cosponsored a bill that would make restrictions on access to pseudoephedrine national law.[1] "There are more sales of cold medicine for illegal uses than legal ones," says Senator Feinstein. "People can go into supermarkets and buy shopping carts full of cold medicine and no one blinks an eye." While some drug firms involved in the $2.2-billion-a-year cold-remedy market oppose

1. The law passed as part of the renewal of the Patriot Act in March 2006.

the bill, several retail chains, including Target and Wal-Mart, moved the most abused cold medicines behind pharmacy counters [in 2005].

The Road to Recovery

To cope with the growing meth epidemic, parents have formed support groups to help one another as well as their kids. Mary Holley, MD, a physician in Arab, Alabama, founded Mothers Against Meth-Amphetamine (MAMA) after her 24-year-old brother became an addict and committed suicide. MAMA, which now has 60 chapters in 30 states, also supports alternative sentencing to jail time (such as community service) for young offenders, as well as greater leeway for schools to order drug testing of students.

Success rates for treating meth addiction vary widely. Thomas Farah, intake director for Second Chances, a recovery program in Statesboro, Georgia, cautions parents not to expect a quick fix. "A few weeks in a detox program will dry out a kid but not fix the addiction," he says. "You have to change your whole life, and that takes a long time." Geared to women of all ages, Second Chances is a 12- to 15-month program that includes counseling, acquisition of job skills, and Bible study. The inflexible structure is not for everyone. One in three addicts drops out, but for graduates, the success rate is 86 percent.

Daniel McGuinn [a pseudonym], a 19-year-old from suburban Phoenix, is living proof that recovery is uncertain at best. Since he began smoking meth as a high school junior, he has been through an inpatient treatment facility in Arizona, a wilderness ranch in Montana, and an extended care facility in California—all to no avail. At home he resisted his parents' best efforts to get him off meth, which included bolting his bedroom window shut so he couldn't sneak out to join his drug buddies. "We couldn't love our son any more than we do," says his mother, 42, a homemaker. "But this drug took over his life and we couldn't control him anymore." Finally, after McGuinn turned 18, his parents kicked him out of the house.

Today he lives alone, works as a telemarketer, and struggles with his meth demons. A few months ago, he went on a meth-smoking spree—evidence of just how hard it is to shake the drug's stranglehold. "We'll all be struggling with this drug for the rest of his life," says McGuinn's mother. "With meth, there are no guarantees."

Compulsive Gambling Is a Growing Problem Among Teens

Monica Villavicencio

Today's young people are the first generation to grow up in a society in which gambling is legal and widely accessible, and as Monica Villavicencio reports in the following selection, the number of gambling youths is growing. From poker games to electronic gambling machines to lotteries and gaming on the Internet, gambling is often touted as a generally harmless form of entertainment. Yet many experts warn that gambling is a high-risk behavior, Villavicencio writes. A growing number of teens, moreover, are developing compulsive gambling habits that are not unlike addictions to tobacco, alcohol, and other drugs. Monica Villavicencio compiled the following report for News-Hour Extra, a production of PBS's NewsHour with Jim Lehrer.

While other addictions such as cigarettes and drugs are fought with warning labels and celebrity ads on TV, parents and educators have not figured out how to reach teens addicted to gambling.

More Teens Are Gambling

Recent studies indicate that more than 70 percent of youth between the ages of 10 and 17 gambled in the past year, up from 45 percent in 1988.

Almost one in three high school students gamble on a regular basis, according to the National Academy of Sciences. Playing cards, the lottery, and scratch tickets as well as betting on sporting events are the most popular forms of gambling among teenagers.

"This is the first generation of kids growing up when gambling is legal and available virtually nationwide," George Meldrum of the Delaware Council on Gambling Problems told CBS News.

Illegal Before 1978

Gambling used to be illegal.

During the early and middle of the 20th century, organized crime syndicates such as the Mafia controlled much of the gambling in the United States, often using it to "launder" (make to appear legal) the profits from other illicit activities, such as drug trafficking.

Nevada had a monopoly over legal casino gambling in the United States until 1978, the year casinos were legalized in Atlantic City, New Jersey.

New Hampshire introduced the first state lottery in 1963 and many states followed suit.

In the past few decades, gambling has grown into a giant corporate industry. Spurred by the legalization of gaming on Native American reservations in the late 1980s, gambling revenues grew from $8 billion to $15 billion from 1988 to 1994.

Seeing the potential for huge profits, more states began to legalize gambling and create lottery games.

Television shows featuring poker tournaments attract high ratings, as does the annual World Series of Poker.

Harmless Entertainment?

Now legal in all but two states, gambling—whether it's the lottery, bingo, or poker night—has gained significant popularity and is seen as a generally harmless form of entertainment.

Researchers say parents do not worry about exposing their children to this habit as they might with alcohol or smoking.

"It is a situation where many parents still do assume that it's better for a kid to be gambling than to be out on the streets doing drugs or whatever," Dr. Rachel Volberg, president of Gemini Research, which specializes in gambling studies, told the *Christian Science Monitor.*

But gambling is addictive. Studies show that problem gamblers exhibit similar functional changes in their brain's decision-making center as drug addicts and alcoholics.

"The neurobiology of what happens when somebody is gambling is much the same as what happens when they are taking cocaine," said gambling addiction expert at the Center for Addiction and Substance Abuse at the University of South Florida Linda Chamberlain on MedicineNet.com.

Researchers have also found that the more exposure a child has to gambling, the more likely he or she will become a compulsive gambler—as a teen and into adulthood.

While 4 percent to 5 percent of adult gamblers will develop a serious gambling problem, underage gamblers are three times as likely as adults to become compulsive gamblers.

Teens' gambling habits can lead to stealing from others and abusing their parents' credit cards.

Researchers at the National Council on Problem Gambling suggest that teens with a gambling problem are more likely to engage in risky behavior such as unsafe sex, binge drinking, smoking marijuana and skipping school.

Gamblers also have the highest suicide rate of any addicted group. In 1997 a 19-year-old New Yorker killed himself, leaving a suicide note blaming a lost $6,000 bet on the World Series.

Addressing the Issue

For underage gamblers, gaining access to gambling outlets is often easier than buying alcohol or cigarettes. The availability of Internet gambling sites makes age regulations increasingly difficult to enforce.

With a growing number of teens at risk of developing compulsive gambling habits, experts are pushing the government to hold hearings to address the issue. They want public service announcements or warning messages to educate the public on the dangers of excessive betting.

"It is a major, growing issue," said Barbara Raimundo, a mother of a recovering gambling addict who now counsels other parents in Connecticut.

"Our youth need major help, and someone has to be willing to step up to the plate before they start getting really devastated."

Prescription Drug Addiction Is a Growing Problem Among Teens

Sandy Fertman Ryan

A new kind of drug abuse is emerging in America: Experts report that in recent years, a rising number of adolescents are using prescription and over-the-counter medications for recreational purposes. According to the Partnership for a Drug Free America, a nonprofit organization dedicated to reducing illicit drug use, teens today are more likely to have abused a prescription drug—including those used to treat attention deficit disorder, painkillers, relaxants, and even cough syrup—than they are to have used illicit street drugs such as cocaine or ecstasy. In the following selection, Sandy Fertman Ryan explores this alarming trend and discusses why girls may be particularly susceptible to this dangerous new type of addiction. Fertman Ryan writes frequently on issues that affect teens.

Lauren [all names have been changed], an honor-roll student from a loving family, battled her weight all through middle school—and it only got worse in high school: "I was so depressed about my body because, every time I was in the hallways, there was always a girl who was skinnier or prettier. I wanted to be the 'hottest' girl. I felt if all the guys were looking at me, it would boost my self-esteem." So when she was 14, Lauren started taking prescription drugs—medications not prescribed to her—in hopes of losing weight and, in her mind, fitting in better at high school.

"The first drug I tried was pot but, about two months later, I started taking Adderall, Concerta and Ritalin, which are all drugs for ADD [Attention Deficit Disorder] or ADHD

[Attention Deficit/Hyperactivity Disorder]. Everyone I knew seemed to have them—either by prescription, or their parents or siblings had them—so they gave them to me. I knew those drugs would decrease my appetite."

Lauren is one of an estimated 14 percent of high-school seniors who've used prescription drugs for non-medicinal purposes. In fact, a whopping one in five U.S. teens has abused Vicodin (a pain reliever), while one in 10 has abused Ritalin and/or Adderall. And the trend toward teens popping pills is increasing at a record pace. Why are so many girls—girls who won't go near illicit drugs like cocaine, ecstasy and heroin—willing to take prescription drugs?

Why Pills, Why Now?

There isn't any one reason girls take pills, but the fact that most families have at least some type of drug, whether over-the-counter or prescribed, so easily accessible in their medicine cabinets is a gigantic influence.

"We live in a world where 5 million school-age children take a prescription drug for behavior disorders, so kids learn at an early age that pills change moods. There are pills all around as they grow up, so they do not see them as anything inherently dangerous," explains Carol Falkowski, director of research communications at the Hazelden Foundation in Minnesota. "Usually, girls who abuse pills are drawn to stimulants that suppress their appetites, because they are so concerned with body image by middle school. There's just so much pressure around them to be thin."

But boredom, rather than weight loss, was the reason Caitlin, 17, took pills. "I started using pills at 16. A lot of my friends were doing it and, since they said they make you feel really relaxed, I wanted to try them. I was so bored with my life at the time, and I really didn't think it was any big deal to take prescription drugs since they're legal.

"The first time I took pills, I had Soma, which is a relaxant. This guy friend of mine gave me two, and I really loved the feeling of just chilling. From then on, I used them as often as I could get my hands on them. That was easy since all of my friends had them, usually from their parents' bathrooms. Pretty soon, I was doing Soma, Vicodin and Valium—all relaxants."

But Caitlin's desire to chill soon became a daily obsession: "My whole day became about what drugs I was going to do and where I was going to get them. I didn't care about anything else." Sure enough, Caitlin's grades took a major dive. "I went from a B average to a D average, which I'd never had before. I was hung over every day, and I constantly felt drowsy. I didn't give a crap about anything except getting high."

Still, how could a teen like Caitlin, raised in an upper-middle class beach community, be bored enough to try drugs? Even Caitlin can't answer that. But Falkowski does: "Kids are overstimulated nowadays, and everything moves so fast—even cartoons move faster than ever. Teens are constantly looking for more stimulation and have a hard time being able to stop and smell the roses."

Summer, 17, describes her experience with pills: "My parents got divorced when I was 3 because of my mom's drug and alcohol use. From then on, I was living two lives. I lived with my dad and was the good girl going to church, but when I'd visit my mom on the weekends. I started doing drugs.

"My mom, little sister and brother all had prescriptions for Adderall. One day, I was watching TV and my mom said she wanted me to help her clean the house—so she gave me Adderall to speed me up. I loved the feeling. From then on, my mom gave me the pills in the morning and after school. If I was upset about something, she'd give me more. If you really need those drugs, they calm you down. But if you don't, like I didn't, they speed you up. Soon, I was up to 12 pills a day, often combining them with other pills. Doing drugs made me feel like I fit in. And watching my mom having such a good time popping pills made me think there was nothing wrong with it."

Many teens assume pills are safe. "Kids see pills all around them, and they get e-mails from people selling them on the Internet, so they assume they're safe and no big deal," says Falkowski. "And very few people get rushed to the emergency room for using prescription drugs, so teens don't see the consequences and therefore assume they're not dangerous."

Teens think that, because prescription drugs are legal, it's no biggie to take them. "Teens don't consider them to be illicit like street drugs," says Kimberly Mitchell-Sellwood, a San Diego-based addictions specialist. But are they really legal? Not when they're prescribed to someone else. . . .

Mitchell-Sellwood adds, "Moms are often the ones who have prescription pills at home, so kids see that modeling and think they're OK to use—even if the prescription isn't for them."

Then, there is the ever-present "I do drugs so I must be cool" factor. "When I was in middle school, it just didn't seem cool to be taking pills as opposed to smoking pot or drinking. But when everyone in high school found out I had pills, suddenly I was cool," says Summer.

Dangers of Doping

Shockingly, a recent study by the Partnership for a Drug-Free America revealed teen abuse of prescription and over-the-counter drugs is just as high or higher than abuse of street drugs.

Summer suggests one reason: "All my friends were smoking pot, but I was too scared to try it. I just always thought of pills as safe, especially if they're prescribed to your brother or sister."

But that just isn't the case. "Prescription drugs can be just as dangerous as street drugs and can set up a lifetime of problems by changing the chemistry in your brain," explains Mitchell-Sellwood.

There are tons of reasons taking pills is just as risky as doing street drugs. For one, they are every bit as addictive. "I don't often see kids addicted to pills only—it's usually a combination of drugs and alcohol that gets out of line. Using drugs like Ritalin absolutely leads to other drugs," says Mitchell-Sellwood. "Teens think, 'If I take one of these and it feels so good, why don't I just feel even better by trying that, too?'"

Prescription drugs can cause serious school, family and friendship problems, as well. "In addition to the long-term consequences, like health risks, there are immediate dangers of impaired judgment, which can affect learning, memory and even driving skills. It can also put you in situations you can't get out of, like sexual or potentially violent situations, because you don't have all of your faculties. Girls get into dangerous situations just in the course of teenage life. If you're under the influence of drugs or alcohol, those situations tend to get even more dangerous," says Falkowski.

Lauren strongly agrees: "I had a physically abusive boyfriend. I would never have been with him had I been sober."

Prescription drugs can also cause serious health problems. Pain medications, like Oxycontin and Vicodin, and relaxants, like Valium and Xanax, can cause potentially fatal breathing problems, among other risks. Stimulants, like Ritalin and Adderall, can cause irregular heartbeats, heart attacks, deadly seizures and psychotic episodes.

Worst of all, when you take a drug that isn't prescribed to you in a way you're not supposed to—by increasing dosages, mixing medications with alcohol or other drugs, or snorting them or injecting them into your bloodstream—you can overdose and put your life at risk. "You don't know with certainty the potency of the pill, the makeup of the pill and what possible interactions it will have with other medications you are taking or allergic reactions that may cause death," explains Falkowski.

Taking prescription drugs recreationally is treacherous territory. It really hits home when you hear the hair-raising experiences of teens like Caitlin: "I bottomed out at age 16. One day, after I'd taken three Somas and two Vicodins, I caught one of my closest friends kissing this guy I was with. I freaked, and then I did something I'd never done in my life—I hit her in the face so hard that I split her lip. Then I just ran to my friend's car, and we drove off.

"The next day in class, the cops showed up, called me out of class, read me my rights and handcuffed me. It was horrible. They drove me to the police station, and I cried the whole time because I was so scared. I had to stay in juvenile hall that night until my parents came to get me. My mind was spinning because I've never been violent before. I didn't know why I would ever hit my friend. I didn't have to go to jail, but I was required to stay clean and under house arrest for three weeks. But right after I was released from house arrest, I was drug-tested by my probation officer—and I flunked. I was immediately taken to a detox center for 21 days."

Summer has her own terrifying story: "After using Ritalin and Adderall on a daily basis, I started taking Oxycontin because I figured, 'No big deal.' But Oxycontin is basically synthetic heroin—you feel so happy and just don't want to move. I'd wake up and not know what I'd done the night before, including having unprotected sex with guys I didn't even know. It was disgusting. I finally bottomed when I was with a friend and we did PCP, Oxycontin and alcohol, along with Ritalin and Adderall. I blacked out for a few days at some guy's house, and my parents eventually found me. The next day, I was sent to rehab."

Popping pills for pleasure can be even more tragic than the consequences Caitlin and Summer experienced. "By age

16," says Lauren, "my life felt totally out of control. I was so depressed, and sick and tired of my life being all about drugs. I was always lying to my parents, trying to keep track of the lies and hiding everything from them. It was exhausting. I had been a straight-A student but, by that point, I had fallen to a 2.4 GPA. I stopped caring about anything but drugs. One day, I cut my wrists to end it all. My parents found me and rushed me to the hospital. They had no idea I was addicted to drugs until that day. Soon after, I was sent to rehab at Hazelden and then to Gables Extended Care. It changed my life. It taught me self-acceptance."

So can Lauren stay off pills for a lifetime? "I want to be successful. I want to be in New York with a briefcase in one hand and a cell phone in the other, and I know I couldn't do that if I were doing any drugs. Instead, I'd be down in an alley trying to score. I take it one day at a time and, if I work this program to my fullest, I can definitely stay sober."

She adds, "The best thing about recovery was finding out I'm not alone. It really gave me hope. I didn't think teens could actually be sober with so much partying going on, but when you meet girls who are—they have jobs, they do well in school, they have great friends—it helps motivate you."

Caitlin, too, is determined to stay sober: "Recovery has been great. I feel so much clearer, so I can do things I love, like surfing. I have been clean for 120 days, and I'm proud of myself. I never wanted to be like my mom, who is still an addict, and yet, when I was using, I was just like her. I can't believe I let that happen. Now, I'm trying to be myself and be a better person and, when I think of my mom, it helps me stay sober."

Summer, who is loving her sober life, feels girls are naive when it comes to taking pills: "All the good girls who get straight A's and want to be perfect think Ritalin will allow them to do all that and more. But they'll just need more and more, and they'll go on to use other drugs for sure. Pills can really ruin your life . . . like they did mine."

CONTEMPORARY
ISSUES
COMPANION

CHAPTER 2

The Causes of Teen Addiction

Genetic Factors Contribute to Teen Addiction

Katherine Ketcham and Nicholas A. Pace

In the following selection Katherine Ketcham and Nicholas A. Pace report that genes play a profound role in the likelihood that a teen will become chemically dependent; that is, children of drug-addicted parents may inherit certain brain abnormalities that predispose them to addiction. The authors explain, for example, that alcoholics are likely to have inherited a deficiency of receptors for dopamine, a brain chemical that makes people feel good. This genetic predisposition, in turn, may drive these individuals to abuse alcohol or other drugs that boost their naturally low dopamine levels. Ketcham and Pace are the authors of Teens Under the Influence: The Truth About Kids, Alcohol, and Other Drugs—How to Recognize the Problem and What to Do About It, *from which the following is excerpted.*

While no one is predestined to become addicted to drugs, we all enter life with varying degrees of vulnerability to drug dependence. Just as some people are more susceptible to diabetes, heart disease, and cancer, so are certain people more physically vulnerable to alcohol and other drug addictions. We inherit this predisposition to certain diseases or disorders from the genes passed down to us by our parents, grandparents, great-grandparents, and on down the line.

Most research studies dealing with the biogenetic aspects of drug addiction focus on the drug alcohol, because beer, wine, and distilled spirits are legal and readily available, and because people (young and old) have been drinking alcohol in one form or another for thousands of years. Almost half of all Americans age twelve or over—109 million people—are current drinkers. More than ten million youths between the ages of twelve and twenty (28.5 percent of that age group) use alcohol, and of this number 6.8 million (19 percent) are considered binge drinkers, drinking five or more drinks on one occasion.

While alcohol is the drug most often studied by researchers, most experts agree that addiction is addiction is addiction no matter what drug is used. Thus, the basic facts about alcohol dependence also hold true for addiction to nicotine, marijuana, cocaine, heroin, methamphetamines, prescription painkillers, tranquilizers, and sedatives, and all other addictive drugs. Different genes and gene combinations are almost certainly involved, but the basic neurological and biological changes that underlie drug addiction remain the same for all addictive drugs.

You don't need to be a geneticist to understand the basic and most essential point underlying addiction—your likelihood of becoming addicted to drugs is determined, in large part, by the genes you inherit from your parents. In alcoholism, for example, we know that the children of alcoholics have a much greater risk of addiction. If one parent is alcoholic, the risk of addiction for the child is approximately 40 percent, or about four times the risk in the general population. If both parents are alcoholics, the risk increases to about 60 percent.

What, exactly, do the children of alcoholics inherit? Multiple genes are involved—perhaps dozens of genes. Some genes may increase the risk of inheriting a predisposition to drug addiction while others decrease the risk, and all these complicated genetic factors interact with various environmental influences to create each individual's unique response to drugs.

We will attempt to simplify the genetic research by focusing on certain key findings. This brief review of the genetic territory can be compared to a quick tour through a foreign country in which you visit only the big cities and popular tourist attractions. . . .

Preference for Alcohol

Tampering with the genetic code of rodents, researchers have created strains of rats and mice that love the taste of alcohol and others that can't stand it. The DBA and C3H strains of mice, for example, consistently prefer water over alcohol when given a choice, while the C57 and C58 strains will choose alcohol over water almost every time. The offspring of the alcohol-loving rodents inherit their parents' fondness for booze, while the descendants of the alcohol-hating mice simply don't like the stuff.

The same thing happens in the world of human beings—some people love the effect of alcohol (even if they can't stand the taste), while others might enjoy a glass of wine or a beer every now and then, and still others have no desire to drink, period.

Animal studies and our own very human experience confirm that genes have a profound effect on *preference*—the desire to drink or abstain from drinking alcohol.

Adoption Studies

In the 1970s, scientists began studying the drinking patterns of adopted children of alcoholics to determine if heredity or environment is most influential in the development of alcoholism. Numerous studies by internationally renowned researchers provide strong confirmation of the genetic link. The important findings generated by this line of research are summarized below:

- Adopted children whose biological parents were alcoholics are *four* times more likely than adopted children of nonalcoholics to become addicted to alcohol.

- Personal contact with the alcoholic biological parent does not affect the likelihood of developing a drinking problem.

- When children whose biological parents were *not* alcoholics are adopted into alcoholic households, they do *not* have an increased risk of alcoholism associated with being raised by alcoholics.

- Adopted children whose biological parents were alcoholics were no more likely to have a psychiatric disturbance than the adopted children whose biological parents were not alcoholics.

Three decades of adoption studies provide clear and unequivocal evidence that predisposition to alcoholism can be passed down from parent to child through the genes. Thus, if you inherit the genes that increase susceptibility to alcoholism, you are significantly more likely to become an alcoholic if you drink.

Brain Wave Abnormalities

In the late 1970s, Henri Begleiter and his colleagues at New York State University in Brooklyn began studying certain brain abnormalities in what is called the P3 brain wave. In a series of studies that continue to this day, Dr. Begleiter's research team discovered that certain deficits in the P3 brain wave exist in alcoholics even many years after they stop drinking.

The researchers then compared the sons of alcoholics, ages seven to thirteen, with the sons of nonalcoholics. Though neither group had ever been exposed to alcohol or other drugs, the sons of alcoholics also had abnormalities in their P3 brain wave.

These electrophysiological "brain marker" studies strongly suggest, in Dr. Begleiter's words, "that decrements in P3 activity are not a consequence of years of heavy drinking but are genetic antecedents of alcohol abuse." In other words, certain brain abnormalities that predispose people to alcoholism are passed from the alcoholic parent to the child—they are part of our genetic inheritance.

Acetaldehyde Buildup

When alcohol is metabolized in the liver, it is converted first to acetaldehyde, a highly toxic (poisonous) substance, and then to acetate. Research teams led by Charles S. Lieber, M.D., have discovered that the same amount of alcohol produces very different blood acetaldehyde levels in alcoholics and non-alcoholics—approximately 50 percent higher in alcoholics. Unfortunately, acetaldehyde is a nasty troublemaker, creating havoc in the liver, the brain, the heart, and other vital organs.

Why are the acetaldehyde levels so much higher in alcoholics? A superefficient metabolic system (called the microsomal ethanol oxidizing system or MEOS) appears to be responsible. Adolescents who are genetically predisposed to alcoholism and who drink heavily and/or regularly may unknowingly set this system into motion, causing the toxic acetaldehyde to build up in the liver. A vicious cycle develops—as alcohol consumption increases, metabolic activity revs up and increased amounts of acetaldehyde are produced, causing damage to the cells responsible for breaking down and eliminating acetaldehyde, which results in more acetaldehyde buildup.

In the liver, a buildup of acetaldehyde causes widespread cell destruction and death. But the damage isn't confined solely to the liver, for some acetaldehyde also travels to the heart, the brain, and other vital organs. In the heart, acetaldehyde inhibits the synthesis of proteins in the heart muscle, which can lead to impaired cardiac functioning. And in the brain, acetaldehyde interacts with certain chemical messengers called neurotransmitters, leading some researchers to theorize that acetaldehyde buildup may be at least partly responsible for the development of neurological addiction and the symptoms of increased tolerance, craving, withdrawal, and progressive loss of control.

Dopamine Deficiencies

Dopamine is a natural brain chemical (neurotransmitter) that makes us feel good. Like its close cousins serotonin, norepinephrine, and GABA [gamma-aminobutyric acid], dopamine is one of many mood-lifting, pleasure-inducing chemical messengers that regularly course through our brains, regulating our moods, reducing compulsive behavior, and generally increasing feelings of well-being.

Some people are born with naturally higher levels of these neurotransmitters than others; they are blessed with an abundance of feel-good chemicals from birth. Other people inherit deficiencies in dopamine and other neurotransmitters; they have less dopamine surging through their brains, which may contribute to chronic feelings of depression, anxiety, irritability, and moodiness.

Alcoholics appear to inherit several genes that influence their natural dopamine levels. In 1990, a team of researchers led by Kenneth Blum, Ph.D., and Ernest Noble, M.D., discovered one gene mutation (the D2 dopamine receptor gene) associated with alcoholism. They theorized that a genetically transmitted defect in this gene leads to deficiencies in dopamine receptors in the brain, which in turn leads to a reduced supply of the feel-good chemical dopamine.

Alcoholics are much more likely to have this genetic abnormality than nonalcoholics, the researchers discovered. Because alcohol works almost instantaneously to open up the dopamine faucets, flooding the brain with the pleasure-creating brain chemical, children who inherit this gene mutation may use alcohol in an attempt to restore a "normal" dopamine balance.

Thus, when kids say they use alcohol in order to feel normal, they may be expressing a scientific truth. For alcohol works quickly and efficiently to raise dopamine levels, thereby creating immediate and intense sensations of pleasure, euphoria, and general well-being. Unfortunately and often tragically, this "wow" reaction to alcohol may be a sign of an underlying chemical imbalance in the brain—which is, in turn, regulated by genetic variations that predispose certain individuals to alcoholism and/or other drug addictions.

The Nature of Brain Development Can Contribute to Teen Addiction

Lee Dye

That high rates of addiction occur during the teen years is incontrovertible, writes Lee Dye in the following article. While a complex set of genetic, social, and other factors accounts for this vulnerability to addiction during the teen years, recent research at Yale University suggests that the nature of adolescent brain development may also be a factor. The parts of the brain that stimulate thrill-seeking behavior, for example, develop early, as opposed to those areas that control decision making and self-control. This brain wiring, Dye reports, may make adolescents more open to experimentation with alcohol and other potentially addictive substances. Dye is a weekly columnist for ABCNEWS .com.

Adolescents who experiment with drugs and alcohol couldn't pick a worse time in their lives to do it.

At that stage in their mental development, the part of the brain that tells them to experiment with drugs is much farther advanced than the part that's supposed to lend a little judgment to the situation.

If they keep going down that path, they may enter their 20s addicted to drugs, partly because addiction may owe as much to the mental developmental agenda as it does to substance abuse.

Doing drugs during the teenage years "really does make concrete changes in the way your brain operates, in a permanent sense," says Andrew Chambers, a Yale University psychia-

Lee Dye, "Study: Teens' Minds Wired for Cheap Thrills," ABCNEWS.com, June 25, 2005. Courtesy of ABCNEWS.com.

trist and lead author of a study in the June [2003] issue of the *American Journal of Psychiatry*.

Chambers and his associates at Yale examined 140 previously completed research projects to see if they could link the various stages of development that adolescents go through with the high rate of addictions that occur early in life.

The Earlier You Start, the Harder It Is to Quit

Most people who can't give up drugs or alcohol or smoking were already addicted in their teenage years, the researchers found. That addiction was due to various causes. Some adolescents have a predisposition toward impulsiveness or recklessness because of genetics or a social situation, making them particularly vulnerable to addiction.

But the researchers also found reason to believe that teenage addiction is partly caused by different rates of development by different parts of the brain. As kids, we look for cheap thrills and exciting adventures, because that's what kids do, and the part of the brain that stimulates that behavior develops very early and rapidly. When we grow up, we're supposed to put away childish things and make mature decisions, but the part of the brain that allows us to do that develops much more slowly.

And that, the researchers conclude, is one reason adolescents and teenagers are more vulnerable to various addictions than any other age group.

The numbers speak for themselves.

"Over 40 percent of adult alcoholics experience alcoholism-related symptoms between ages 15 and 19, and 80 percent of all cases of alcoholism begin before age 30," the researchers report in their paper. "The median reported age of initiation of illicit drug use in adults with substance use disorders is 16 years, with 50 percent of cases beginning between ages 15 and 18 and rare initiation after age 20."

The list goes on. Most adult smokers began before the age of 18. And the earlier the kids get into drugs, the stronger the addiction, and the greater the morbidity.

The Importance of Dopamine

Why people use these dangerous substances, and why we sometimes become addicted, is a very complex mosaic of human development, social pressures, genetics and other factors that produce a very incomplete picture. As Chambers himself notes, not everybody who does drugs or drinks booze as an adolescent goes down the tubes. Some people outgrow it, so whatever brain damage occurred early on, if any, didn't leave them permanently crippled.

"A lot of people do use a lot of drugs or alcohol when they are in their late teens and early 20s and come out OK," he says. As a college professor, he knows not all those students are spending all their time buried in books.

"Man, there's a lot of partying that most people go through in college," he says, "and most of those people make it out of that and settle down into non-substance-disordered patterns."

But a lot of them don't, and the reasons are not yet clear.

The researchers focused on the release of dopamine in the brain, which operates "like a general 'go' signal," they report. Drugs, sex, even video games release dopamine, stimulating the brain and making us want more. But lots of other things also generate dopamine.

Food and even stress and trauma also release dopamine, and that has set researchers off in a new direction. Dopamine isn't just released by rewarding things. It's also released by events or circumstances that may threaten our survival or way of life.

Inhibition Comes Too Little Too Late

So it isn't all about "reward and pleasure," Chambers says. Since dopamine is released by a wide variety of stimuli, there must be some common ground between such things as drugs, food, sex and stress. That common denominator, many scientists believe today, is motivation.

Motivation can either pull us back from dangerous substances, like addictive drugs, if our "mature" side of mental development is on the job, or it can push us farther into harm's way, if the kid is still in charge.

Getting high, or taking a risk, is an early motivation among adolescents who are eager to try out their walking shoes. But a little later, motivation should shift somewhat as the part of the brain that inhibits impulses matures.

But by that time, addiction may have already set in.

It's not easy being a kid.

Contemporary American Culture Contributes to Teen Addiction

Stanton Peele

The popular notion that addiction is a physical disease is patently false, according to Stanton Peele, a psychologist who specializes in addiction. In truth, writes Peele in the following article, young people exhibit addictive behavior in response to social factors: The primary activity of a vast number of American children and adolescents, for example, is the passive consumption of media, a pastime that may supersede the powerful life experiences and personal relationships that are necessary for healthy human development. The result, Peele contends, is a large populace of disconnected and dissatisfied youth who are extremely susceptible to addictive or other destructive urges. Peele has written many books on addiction, including Love and Addiction, Diseasing of America, *and* Seven Tools to Beat Addiction.

We live in an era that creates addiction, which our culture chooses to regard as a disease. Yet, underlying the remarkable and never-decreasing incidence of compulsive, self-destructive behavior, is our addictogenic culture. That is, our culture in its most basic elements encourages addiction. To understand this is to take a powerful step towards improving the emotional health of our children and ourselves. Yet, it is in the nature of such basic cultural patterns that it is difficult to separate ourselves sufficiently to perceive how our culture shapes us.

Stanton Peele, "Combating the Addictogenic Culture," October 22, 2005. www.peele .net. Reproduced by permission.

Immunization for Drug Abuse

To see how wrong-headed is our approach to addiction, consider that a popular recent topic in the drug treatment world has been immunization against addiction. Those who have shown susceptibility to drug use might be thus immunized—or else, considering that majorities of high school youths who will eventually experiment with drugs and, certainly, alcohol—all youths might be vaccinated.

What does immunization for drug abuse look like? National Institute on Drug Abuse researchers have formulated a compound that reduces the amount of cocaine that enters the brains of rats. Presumably, those who are thus vaccinated will become immune to the stimulant effects of the drug.

However, could these same individuals turn to amphetamines (including crystal meth), or simply cigarettes, for stimulant effects? Or might they rely on Ritalin—a stimulant prescribed for children with attention deficit disorder (ADD) and hyperactivity? Or could they become addicted to something that many children now spend a great deal of time on—video games?

Of course, stimulant drugs are only one variety of substances to which people could become addicted, and to which kids can turn. Marijuana is now a popular object of concern—and alcohol affects many more children than all illicit drugs combined.

But there are other, legal drugs that children might learn to rely on—and that our entire culture has increasingly become dependent on. The chief of these is antidepressants. That is, the World Health Organization has characterized antidepressant drugs as addictive, since they produce withdrawal effects. Yet, more and more Americans rely on antidepressants. At the same time, kids are the fastest-growing segment of the antidepressant market.

Despite the advent of antidepressants, depression in our society is not abating, and is especially evident among the young. Why are more people dissatisfied with their lives, and feeling insufficient to cope with the demands on them—or that the emotional rewards they receive are not adequate. As I have described in books from *Love and Addiction* to *7 Tools to Beat Addiction*, addiction is a search for gratification that is not otherwise available to people.

Predisposed to Addiction?

Where does addiction stem from and how does it manifest itself? What if children are becoming more predisposed to addiction due to the very nature of their lives in America, leading to successively more addicted generations of Americans? For example, if addiction is a fundamentally dependent way of relating to life, might young people who have less independent exposure to the world be more likely to seek other forms of addiction?

In the end, it is not exposure to this substance or that, prescribed medicine or street drug, that causes addiction. It is failure to engage in the world, to believe in one's competence and ultimate chance for success, and to care enough for people, things, and oneself to eschew self-destructive behavior.

In other words, if children feel incapable of exploring and coping with their own worlds; if their experiences are constantly monitored and mediated by adults; if their primary activities involve passive consumption of media—might they become susceptible to any of a range of addictions? And then they may find a wide variety of objects for their addictive urges—cocaine, or other stimulant drugs, or other illicit drugs, or other drugs (prescribed as well as illicit), or other powerful, absorbing experiences.

In *Love and Addiction*, I wrote with my colleague Archie Brodsky, "Addiction is not an abnormality in our society. It is not an aberration from the norm; it is itself the norm." While we warn children constantly about the dangers of drugs and alcohol, we may at the same time actually be prompting them to become addicted and to abuse substances, from prescribed medications to food (the Surgeon General has identified rapidly growing childhood overweight and obesity as America's number one public health problem).

But, as we noted in *Love and Addiction*, addictive urges can permeate and determine all of our activities, involvements, and relationships. If we do not find our lives sufficiently engaging, then we can find addiction in any direction that we turn. And we will.

A Variety of Factors Puts Teens at Risk for Addiction

Timmen L. Cermak

In the following selection author and psychologist Timmen L. Cermak explores the complex interplay of biological, social, developmental, emotional, and familial factors that may contribute to a teen's susceptibility to marijuana dependence—and addictions in general. To Cermak, the single most powerful predictor of a teen's risk for developing addiction is genetics; that is, whether a blood relative has or had a history of addiction. Other factors that may have a profound impact on addictive behavior include disconnected families, psychiatric disorders, and community norms. Cermak has written extensively on the subject of addiction, and the following is excerpted from his book Marijuana: What's a Parent to Believe?

Life is not fair, and the inequality of life as it relates to addiction is significant and multilayered. There are genetic differences at the core of every cell. There are neurological differences peppered throughout our brains. And there are profound environmental differences, including the families we are born to, the neighborhoods surrounding our families, and the culture surrounding those neighborhoods. All these influences powerfully affect our overall life experience financially, socially, educationally, spiritually, and physically. And they also powerfully affect any individual's risk of developing chemical dependence. . . .

Genetics

The most fundamental risk factor for marijuana addiction (and addiction in general) is genetics. Genetic susceptibility to addiction forms a firm cornerstone of our current under-

Timmen L. Cermak, from *Marijuana: What's a Parent to Believe?* Center City, MN: Hazelden, 2003, pp. 77–93. © 2003 by Hazelden Foundation. All rights reserved. Reprinted by permission of Hazelden Foundation.

standing of addiction as a disease. The single most powerful predictor of any individual's risk for developing addiction is a positive family history—a parent, grandparent, uncle, or aunt who is chemically dependent. . . .

Parental addiction is not a sure predictor of who will become harmfully involved with pot. Not all children, not even the majority, with addicted parents become addicted. And teens with no known family history of addiction certainly can become addicted. But if we had only one question to ask to find the group of adolescents who run the highest risk of problems with marijuana, it would be to ask who has a parent who is abusing, or dependent on, any chemicals.

Living with a Substance-Abusing or Addicted Parent

Not only are teens with an abusing or addicted parent at greater risk for inheriting a genetic predisposition to addiction, but living with a parent who is harmfully involved with alcohol or other drugs also teaches a host of lessons. It teaches that adults normally respond to emotional distress by resorting to chemicals. It recruits kids into the same denial that already shrouds the parent from the truth about his or her illness. It teaches kids to hide the truth from the world outside the family, to lie, to cover their family shame, and to remain "loyal" to a parent by acting as though nothing is wrong.

Living with an addicted parent can also teach kids that nothing in the world is really predictable. It teaches children that they are ultimately on their own. No one can ever be counted on to protect them. Chaos and despair simply need to be lived with. Emotional needs come second. It teaches many kids to harden their hearts and not let anyone in, to avoid being hurt even further. It teaches children not to trust. . . .

Presence of a Psychiatric Problem

A third important risk factor for adolescent problems with marijuana is the presence of a separate psychiatric problem, such as attention deficit hyperactivity disorder, clinical depression, conduct disorder, social anxiety, post-traumatic stress disorder, or specific learning disorders. A psychiatric problem, very often preceding any drug use, can be found in 83 percent of teens who satisfy the criteria for marijuana dependence, in 46 percent of those with marijuana abuse, and in only 29 percent of occasional users. In some cases, teens may use marijuana in an effort to cope with underlying problems; in other cases, smoking can trigger the onset of psychiatric difficulties. In either case, being high usually intensifies psychiatric problems. In general, more severe psychiatric problems and more severe marijuana addiction are associated with one another.

Attention Deficit Disorder

Attention deficit disorder (ADD) is one of the most common problems I see in teens with marijuana dependence. They generally come into my office convinced that pot is the perfect medicine for their disordered attention span. The two effects of marijuana that they cite as benefits are that it calms them down (physically and emotionally) and it focuses their attention. Then they usually throw in, "It's all natural and God's gift to humans. Besides, the drugs doctors use are unnatural and have more harmful side effects." From their defense of marijuana, I can tell that they have gone beyond being seduced by its effects and have become devoted to its use. For teenage boys, especially, with hyperactive forms of ADD, marijuana is most often the drug of choice because their physical hyperactivity is often the primary cause of classroom problems. . . .

Depression

Depression is now recognized as common among adolescents. The National Institute of Mental Health (NIMH) estimates that 8 percent of teens suffer from depression. Fully three million teens meet the criteria for a diagnosis of clinical depression. The darkness, irritability, and despair they experience grinds no less deeply than in adults suffering from depression. Unfortunately, teen depression is less often recognized, because sufferers are usually not in a position to seek medical/psychological help on their own and adults have difficulty distinguishing their symptoms from the emotional volatility normally seen in adolescents. Those whose depression stems from childhood trauma—physical, emotional, and/or sexual—may even avoid seeking the professional help they need in order to protect family members who perpetrated the abuse. For these kids, the feelings of isolation and alienation that are an inherent part of depression are intensified by their family's denial.

A host of other factors leads to the overwhelming level of stress experienced by teens and their families today. Parents who work long hours or who are unable to find enough work to provide a secure home can stress teens as well. Divorce, single parenting, and remarriages can all create tension in kids. Competition for good colleges, good high schools, and even for the "best" kindergartens has robbed childhood of much of the down time that it used to have. Stranger abductions, the latest missing children on the nightly news, and terrorism on our own shores surround teens with an atmosphere of fear. Washboard abs, thin runway models, and perfect skin all seem necessary for acceptance. If teens aren't stressed out, some of us may wonder what's wrong with them. The demands put on hurried teens today and the unrealistic expectations they hold for themselves have produced levels of stress, and therefore levels of depression, unseen in past generations.

When depression is not recognized or treatment is not available, marijuana often is. The temporary mood elevation that comes with getting high is a relief to some adolescent sufferers of depression. But the elevated mood soon becomes more a memory than a reality. After the high wears off, the emotional slump that follows adds its weight to the underlying depression. They continue to smoke pot in hopes of recapturing the initial euphoria they experienced. . . .

Family Values

Certain aspects of an adolescent's family environment have been identified as increasing the risk for early and heavy marijuana use.

Families with moralistic, rigid, and extreme views about alcohol and other drugs breed more drug use by their children than do families with moderate views. This is true whether the extreme views favor or oppose drug use. In either case, the family has invested chemicals with a lot of emotional charge, and this charge gets passed on to their children. Moderation breeds moderation. Extremes increase risk.

Families that maintain their rituals and celebrations experience less drug abuse among their children. Routines such as family meals, vacations, and even shared regular chores create cohesion and provide ballast for youngsters. Families that maintain connections to their spiritual heritage and provide their children with some spiritual training decrease the risk of drug abuse. Celebrations of birthdays, anniversaries, and national holidays increase a sense of being important and honored in one's family. And cultural rituals such as those surrounding Christmas, Hanukkah, Kwanza, reunions, weddings, and funerals all help children feel connected to a broader world.

Supply vs. Demand

Oddly enough, the ready availability of marijuana does not necessarily increase an adolescent's risk of marijuana abuse. To illustrate the lack of direct relationship between marijuana availability and use we need only look at two trends. In 1978, approximately 50 percent of high school seniors had smoked pot during the previous twelve months. This fell to less than 25 percent by 1991 and has since risen to just shy of 40 percent. Throughout this entire time, however, the number of seniors who reported that it was easy to obtain pot held steadily between roughly 82 to 86 percent. . . .

What *has* varied with increases and decreases of marijuana use is people's perceptions of its harmfulness. . . . The more harmful people see marijuana to be, the fewer people [who] smoke, despite its unchanged availability. In other words, demand reduction appears to be more effective than supply reduction.

Community Norms

The community norms surrounding adolescents can have a profound impact on whether they try marijuana. While many communities want drug prevention to be taken care of at the schools, the problem is not isolated to school-age children. When communities wink at the adults' use of marijuana or tolerate other drug usage, the children absorb this message. Kids really do what their parents do, not what they say. Kids only pretend to do what parents say so they can do what parents do behind their backs. Nearly every community across America contains an adult drug-friendly subculture. Near my hometown, out on the Pacific Coast, lies an isolated community of old hippies. I have heard kids from that community complain when they were arrested for marijuana possession that they did not know it was illegal. Few, if any, in their home community ever object to its use or treat it as illegal.

While this is an extreme example, it illustrates a reality that exists in lesser forms in every community. I know too many lawyers, doctors, police officers, teachers, and school board members who still occasionally smoke marijuana not to understand that its use pervades every community. Trying to delay or prevent marijuana use among teenagers cannot be divorced from the community's norms as a whole. Without involvement of the whole community, school-based drug prevention programs are both hypocritical and doomed to be ineffective. The entire community has a stake in delaying and preventing teen use of marijuana. And the community's norms are a prime component of what must be openly discussed if this goal is ever to be reached.

The Gateway Effect of Tobacco and Marijuana

Henry David Abraham

Tobacco, marijuana, and other misdemeanor drugs are referred to as gateway drugs because many people who experiment with them will progress to using felony drugs such as cocaine or heroin. According to Henry David Abraham, not all kids experimenting with marijuana will move on to harder drugs yet Abraham does believe that there is a correlation between smoking cigarettes and the later use of marijuana and other drugs. Daily cigarette smokers, Abraham notes, have a tenfold increase in risk of using marijuana and cocaine. Abraham is a psychiatrist and the author of What's a Parent to Do? Straight Talk on Drugs and Alcohol, *from which the following is excerpted.*

Jason's father, a hard-driving litigator [lawyer], had steadily provided his family with a six-figure income. Jason did not want for anything: private school, costly camps, a lovely upscale suburban home. Unfortunately, his learning disorder was not picked up at home or his private school. He was eleven when he took to smoking cigarettes in the tool shed in his spacious backyard. Losing interest in school, he also lost the anxiety of being caught smoking by his parents and began smoking before and after school with his friends.

He enjoyed no team sports, had increasingly poor grades and no apparent interest in after-school activities except skateboarding. His mood at home was sullen, angry and depressed. So when a friend offered him some marijuana as a pick-me-up, his response was "Cool!" Pot soon became a crutch to get through the day. He found that school was becoming a hostile

Henry David Abraham, from *What's a Parent to Do?: Straight Talk on Drugs and Alcohol.* Far Hills, NJ: New Horizon Press, 2004, pp. 25–29. Copyright © 2004 by Henry David Abraham, M.D. All rights reserved. Reproduced by permission of the Bobbe Siegel Agency.

and inexplicable territory, which he dealt with by a cycle of playing hooky and smoking, until he left school permanently at sixteen. His father tried to get him jobs, but he held them erratically, since the trail of marijuana followed him wherever he went.

When the marijuana started to lose its magic, Jason found the idea of heroin intriguing, especially when his friends promised there would be "no needles." At his first snort, he felt nauseated and then mellow for the first time in memory. Over the next few months, heroin became his new best friend. When he didn't have it on hand, withdrawal became his most frightening enemy. One night a drug buddy showed him how to shoot the drug and he told himself the biggest lie an addict can tell himself. He "had to do what he had to do."

In no time, Jason was into his dealer for a several-hundred-dollar-a-week habit. To support it, he began to steal, at first from his family, then his friends and, finally, from neighbors' homes when they were on vacation. When pickings were slim, he graduated to armed robbery. His recovery from addiction only began after he was wounded during an attempted robbery of a pharmacy for Oxycontin, a narcotic pain reliever.

The Gateway Theory

Jason's story exhibits a number of common milestones in the stumble to addiction. Starting with legal drugs (tobacco), users progress to misdemeanor drugs (marijuana) and then to felony drugs (heroin). This is known as "the gateway theory," an important finding of Professors Denise Kandel at Columbia and Gene Smith at Harvard, among others. Thankfully, the majority of kids who take the first step or two do not go farther.

This fact has led to some misunderstanding of what the gateway idea is all about. This hypothesis flags certain behaviors that increase *the risk* of addiction. It does not predict that *all* kids experimenting with legal or misdemeanor drugs will progress inexorably to felony drugs, anymore than skydiving always leads to crash landings.

Let's do some of the numbers. This work is by researchers Andrew Golub and Bruce Johnson and was published in 2001 in the *American Journal of Public Health*. If you track 100,282 people for eighteen years (exhausted yet?) to at least until age twenty-six, you find that roughly 85 percent of them use alcohol or tobacco at some point in their lives. 21.7 percent of the 100,000 proceeded to add marijuana use to the list and 7.7 percent proceeded to add hard drugs. However, these researchers also noted that an increasing number of hard drug users did *not* follow the gateway path, particularly inner city kids.

So where does that leave us with the gateway theory? Marijuana use, especially heavy use, counts as a predictor for moving on to hard stuff, but it is hardly the whole story. What does this say about our public war against marijuana use? Our leaders reasoned that if we stamped out marijuana, following the predictions of the gateway theory, other drug abuse would be stamped out as well. So far, so bad. This policy, which has inspired the spending of literally billions of tax dollars in the War on Drugs, is reminiscent of the drunk who loses his keys at night and insists on looking for them under a lamppost, because that's where the light is. The policy also shifts the responsibility of drug prevention the wrong way, from parents, where it should be, to law enforcement authorities, where it shouldn't. There are *many factors* that lead a kid into hard drugs, not just the softer ones. . . .

[One] will quickly recognize that anyone's ability to predict anything about the future seldom gets high marks for accuracy. And so a certain degree of humility is indicated when we claim to be able to predict which kids are likely to use drugs in the future. We simply cannot know *with certainty* if our concerns will be borne out. . . .

Finally, let me make a distinction between drug experimentation, drug abuse and addiction. The first occurs because kids want to know what all this drug and alcohol fuss is about. They want to be like their peers, regress from the adulthood pressures that loom before them or become adventurers of the mind. However, the last two, abuse and addiction, are trouble. . . .

What Kids Do to Increase the Chance of Drug Abuse

This one is easy: they smoke cigarettes. Far and away this one behavior predisposes to later use of marijuana and hard stuff. It makes sense. Aside from knowing how to eat a marijuana brownie, you have to know how to smoke to use marijuana. Smoking cigarettes is a gateway to marijuana. It is also the earliest addiction. What follows, not *always*, I must add, is that the gateway effect of marijuana is to stronger stuff like LSD and cocaine. Daily cigarette smokers have a ten-fold increase in risk of using marijuana and cocaine. Other big red flags for future drug use are delinquency, cutting class at school and alcohol use in all three forms—beer, wine and liquor.

An important point regarding the use of gateway drugs (alcohol, marijuana and tobacco) is that the younger a kid starts, the more serious the eventual outcome becomes. For example, a kid who smokes pot before the age of twelve is forty-two times more likely to use cocaine or heroin than a kid who first came to pot after age sixteen.

Marketing Tobacco and Alcohol to Teens

Susan Linn

According to Susan Linn, the alcohol and tobacco industries depend on alcoholics and heavy smokers for a large portion of their profits. Children, then, are absolutely essential to these industries; tobacco companies, for example, need to cultivate new smokers to replace the 440,000 who die each year. To hook their next generation of lifelong customers, writes Linn, these companies focus their marketing efforts on adolescents through a variety of methods. Linn is a psychologist and the author of Consuming Kids: The Hostile Takeover of Childhood, *from which the following is excerpted.*

Children are important to the alcohol and the tobacco industries. According to the National Institute on Alcohol Abuse, people who start drinking before the age of fifteen are four times more likely to develop a dependency on alcohol than those who start drinking when they're twenty-one. Lifetime alcohol abuse and dependence is greatest for those who begin drinking between the ages of eleven and fourteen (or younger), and the alcohol industry depends on alcoholics for a significant portion of their profits. In combination, adults who drink excessively and underage drinkers account for almost half of all alcohol sales in the United States. Tobacco companies need to keep creating smokers to replace the 440,000 who die each year, so it's essential for business that they get children to start smoking. The younger children are when they begin to smoke, the more likely it is that they will become regular smokers and the less likely that they will ever successfully quit. If a person can reach the age of twenty without beginning to smoke, he or she has almost no likelihood of starting. Ninety percent of smokers began before they turned eighteen.

It's illegal to sell alcohol to anyone under twenty-one. It's illegal to sell cigarettes to children under eighteen. When it comes to marketing to children, the alcohol industry periodically comes under government scrutiny and, in 1998, the tobacco industry became subject to some government regulations. Yet children and teenagers continue to be targets for marketing by both industries.

A Dangerous Trend

There is significant public health concern about children's consumption of alcohol and tobacco—enough so that consumption of each is tracked through more than one ongoing government survey of risky behaviors among youth. For all the similarities between the two, there are differences as well. Tobacco is inherently addictive and harmful to adults as well as children, even when used as intended. While alcohol can be addictive, it is certainly possible for many people to drink in what alcohol abuse counselors call "low-risk ways" without harming themselves. On the other hand, of the approximately 9.7 million drinkers between twelve and twenty, close to 20 percent engage in binge drinking and 6 percent are heavy drinkers. By about seventh grade, 20 percent of students have tried alcohol. By eighth grade, that figure rises to 50 percent.

Alcohol is implicated in four of the leading causes of adolescent deaths, including automobile accidents, suicide, homicide, and unintentional injuries. Researchers estimate that alcohol is involved in one-third to two-thirds of adolescent "date rapes" and sexual assaults. Almost 30 percent of fifteen- to seventeen-year-olds say that alcohol or drugs influenced their decision to engage in sexual activity. About one quarter of that same group said that drugs or alcohol caused them to do more sexually than they intended or were comfortable with.

When it does not employ animated amphibians, today's alcohol advertising grabs the attention of teens and preteens by exploiting the same vulnerabilities as ads for clothing or accessories. Populated by ever-so-slightly-older beautiful people, these ads offer the promise of an ever-so-fun-filled life brimming with sex, lack of bothersome inhibition, and raucous parties, all centered around alcohol—mostly beer, although hard liquor is marketed to young people as well. All your loneliness, insecurities, or awkwardness will disappear, these ads promise, with a Bud, or a Coors Light, or a Heineken. Kids are getting the message. Most of them drink not because they like the taste, but to relax, to feel more mature, be more uninhibited, or because it's supposed to be fun.

Alcohol companies swear that they are targeting twenty-one to thirty-four-year-olds, but the themes and media techniques that characterize beer advertising, for instance, have undeniable appeal for teens as well. For example, the industry has a self-imposed rule that models in commercials need to be at least twenty-five, but as we know from the way marketers characterize teens and tweens as "aspirational," models who look old enough to be in their twenties have great appeal to teenagers. Besides, many of the models in beer commercials I've seen look young enough to be under twenty-one. The themes or stories portrayed in some alcohol commercials seem more relevant to underage drinkers than anyone else. . . .

Widespread Exposure to Alcohol Advertising

Thanks to major grants from large foundations such as Robert Wood Johnson Foundation and the Pew Charitable Trusts, we are beginning to accumulate more data about adolescent exposure to alcohol advertising. Kids—particularly those who watch sports on television—are inundated with alcohol ads. Alcohol companies reach teens (and preteens and—as we shall see—even young children) through commercials on television and radio and in magazines. They also reach children through media promotions, product placement in movies and television programs, and through sponsoring sports events and rock concerts.

Teens (including twelve-year-olds) see more commercials for alcohol on television than they do for skin-care products, jeans, and snacks like potato chips. In 2001, alcohol companies spent over $31 million on ads during thirteen of the fifteen most popular shows among kids twelve to seventeen, including *Friends, That '70s Show,* and *Survivor Africa.* Many of these shows are also watched by younger kids. According to A.C. Nielsen data, on average more than 2.1 million kids between two and eleven watched *Survivor Africa* each week. Over 1.3 million were watching weekly episodes of *Friends.*

In 2001, the alcohol industry reached 89 percent of teens who watch television. The average teen viewer saw 245 alcohol commercials on the tube that year. Teens who are heavy viewers saw more than three times that amount. They are also more likely to drink. A study from Stanford Medical school showed that the more television kids watched in ninth grade, the more likely they were to have begun drinking eighteen months later. The likelihood increased 9 percent for each hour of television watched.

Of course, television commercials represent only a fraction of the total amount of advertising to which kids are exposed. The industry spent about $218 million on radio advertising last year [2003], up from $176 million in 2000, with 81 percent of those millions coming from the beer industry. The Center for Alcohol Marketing and Youth at Georgetown University found that almost 40 percent of radio ads monitored in 2002 were aired on stations favored by teens. Commercials for certain brands of beer, such as Budweiser and Coors Light, were more likely to be heard by twelve- to twenty-year-olds than by adults aged twenty-one to thirty-four.

The alcohol industry also advertises in magazines popular with teens. In 2001, ten magazines that have a significant youth readership, *Vibe, Spin, Rolling Stone, Allure, Car and Driver, Maxim, Glamour, Motor Trend, In Style,* and *Sports Illustrated,* accounted for almost one-third of alcoholic beverage advertising in magazines. Topping this list in spending on alcohol ads is *Sports Illustrated,* which took in $31 million in alcohol advertising that year and was reported to have a youth readership of 6,127,000 in 2001.

Among the alcohol brands advertising in these magazines are "alcopops," or "malternatives," such as Doc Otis' Hard Lemonade Malt Beverage and Smirnoff Ice Premium Malt Beverage. Malternatives are marketed as "low-alcohol refreshers," but actually they contain more alcohol than beer. Teenagers see 60 percent more print ads for malternatives than do adults over the age of twenty-one.

The ads themselves are particularly attractive to teens. For instance, a Sam Adams beer commercial shows a young guy in the midst of a large party lying to a cop who is responding to a complaint about noise. The camera lovingly follows this guy's hand as he hides his beer bottle behind his back. "Uh, you must have the wrong address," he says. This ad brilliantly plays into adolescent identity issues—feeding into a defy-authority, us-against-them mentality. The viewer is definitely rooting for the kids and not the cop. . . .

Tobacco Marketing

As I said earlier, tobacco differs from most other legal products, including alcohol, because it is harmful even when used as intended. It has the dubious honor of being the subject of the very first public health treaty ever issued by the World Health Organization [WHO], designed to limit the spread of smoking. One way WHO intends to do that is to restrict advertising. How they will enforce the treaty remains to be seen. Aside from greed or adherence to extreme libertarian beliefs, it's hard to understand why tobacco continues to be marketed to anyone anywhere, let alone to children. But it does. And tobacco marketing is effective, especially with kids. Eighty-six percent of teen smokers smoke Camels, Newports, or Marlboros—the most heavily advertised brands.

In 1998, after years of public health research, advocacy, and lawsuits, the American tobacco industry and forty states signed a Master Settlement Agreement in which, among other things, the industry agreed to stop intentionally marketing to kids. Within two years, the amount of money spent on advertising tobacco increased by 42 percent. A year later my friend Zoe called me in my office, outraged that her thirteen-year-old daughter had just received a catalogue in the mail from a company selling all sorts of cigarette paraphernalia such as hats, backpacks, and T-shirts. Last week I walked into a convenience store across the street from my daughter's old elementary school. It's a store where kids stop in to buy candy and soda. Among the cigarette advertisements were those for a variety of flavored brands from Camel—mirroring the same flavors as candy, or chapstick.

The cigarette companies may have changed the ways they do it, but they are still marketing to children. A look at some of the internal documents generated by the tobacco industry from before the settlement explains why, in the words of tobacco executives. A memo from Philip Morris (now Altria) says, "Today's teenager is tomorrow's potential regular customer ... the smoking patterns of teenagers are particularly important to Philip Morris." According to an executive from R.J. Reynolds, "Evidence is now available to indicate that the 14–18-year-old group is an increasing segment of the smoking population, RJR-T must soon establish a successful new brand in this market if our position in the industry is to be maintained in the long term." Perhaps it's the executive from Lorillard who summed it up best: "[T]he base of our business is the high school student." In other words, if tobacco companies stop marketing to kids, the industry goes up in smoke.

Middle-Class Teens Are Susceptible to Addiction

Elliott Currie

According to Elliott Currie, the culture that surrounds many middle-class teens is one in which an individual's value is contingent on meeting certain standards of performance—in academics and athletics, for example. This emphasis on competitive success, and the high stress level it engenders, may breed many forms of deviant adolescent behavior. Currie describes how, for example, adolescents faced with impossibly high expectations may find the drug world comforting and even empowering—a respite, perhaps, from the intolerable feelings of failure, inadequacy, and defeat. Currie is a professor of criminology and law at the University of California at Irvine and the author of The Road to Whatever: Middle-Class Culture and the Crisis of Adolescence, *from which the following is excerpted.*

A ... theme in the family lives of many troubled middle-class adolescents is what I call the problem of contingent worth. By that I mean that the culture that surrounds them is one in which individuals' value—in their own eyes and those of others—is, to an unusual extent, conditional on their meeting certain narrow standards of performance. It is not sufficient to be simply a "good kid"—or to be hardworking, courageous, or generous, all qualities that might be expected to give adolescents a firm sense that they are fundamentally worthwhile. Instead, too much rides on their ability to rank high on just a few scales of worth, which, in the American middle class, typically involve some sort of competitive achievement—outdoing others in school, sports, or whatever arena is considered most important in the struggle for status and prestige.

For adolescents who grow up in the culture of contingent worth, it is rarely good enough merely to do well; they have to do better than others. As a result, there is always hanging over their heads the worry that someone out there is doing even better. . . .

The fundamental problem for youth raised in such a culture is that not everyone can beat everyone else: only a few can win even most of the time. Thus, this value system sets up most of its adherents for failure. Where personal worth is necessarily a scarce commodity, there will inevitably be a great many people who think of themselves as relatively worthless. Every culture, to be sure, has standards by which its members are ranked, and in every culture it is possible to fail, to fall short. But what is unusual about the culture in which many American adolescents grow up is how narrowly the standards of success are drawn and how total the effect of failing to meet them can be, how completely one is defined by one's relative position in this competitive struggle for preeminence. There is no natural limit to the number of children who can be loyal, honest, caring, or many other things that a less constricted culture might deem important and worthy of respect. But in a struggle *against* others—a struggle to be on top in just one dimension or two of life—many must lose, and some must lose badly. And when they do, there are few alternative sources of self-respect to turn to. . . .

It could be argued that the psychological pressures bred by the uniquely American emphasis on competitive success are actually worse for the children of the middle class, precisely because there are fewer external barriers they can point to as explanations or justifications for their inability to make it to the highest rungs of a narrow ladder of social performance. Poor youth can—and often do—point to discrimination or lack of resources or connections to explain why they haven't done more or done better. Middle-class adolescents are largely denied those structural excuses and are indeed typically taught to blame themselves for their real or imagined failure to stand out in the realms where their performance is most crucially judged—school, athletics, social status. . . .

The problem of how to cope with losing, accordingly, is a pervasive and pressing one in mainstream American culture— and especially so for adolescents, because they are in the midst of an already tricky and sometimes painful process of defining who they are. . . .

One way to cope with the potentially intolerable sense of being worthless and a loser is to stop caring—or to try with all your might to find ways not to care, to block the nagging pain and humiliation of feeling yourself a failure in the eyes of those whose opinion most matters. Another is to change the frame of reference—to look outside your family and community for approval and respect—or to change the terms of the game by challenging the legitimacy of the ranking system itself and replacing it with a new one. . . . This strategy can help adolescents escape from feelings of failure and despair and begin to turn their lives around. But it can also work the other way: the search for alternative sources of approval and esteem can lead them to dangerous places indeed.

In contrast to [teens] whose parents essentially abandoned responsibility for their well-being, the teenagers most affected by the culture of invidious ranking usually face a different, though related, problem at home. Their parents are, on the whole, more competent and are often quite successful in conventional terms. And they are, in their own way, more involved with their children—more likely to monitor their behavior and to engage in what the sociologist Annette Larreau calls "concerted cultivation." But they do so in ways that profoundly undermine their children's sense of being capable people whose lives count for much. Among the adolescents I spoke with, those who grew up in such families were often the ones who, when they fell, fell the hardest and fastest.

"I Was Pretty Much a Nice Kid"

I met Rick a year or so after he had stopped drinking himself into unconsciousness several nights a week. Bright, engaging, and talented, he grew up in an affluent suburb with parents who were both driven, successful businesspeople. But by the middle of high school he'd gotten to the point where he would regularly drink until he blacked out and would wake up barely remembering what else he'd done. "I ended up getting a reputation," he says. "Actually I don't really like running into people from high school because they remember me as 'that guy who can drink.'"

Rick describes himself, along with many of his equally hard-drinking high school friends, as having been "lost and confused" and profoundly unhappy in those years; they were really not, he says, "bad kids." He started drinking because it seemed like people who drank had fun, and he wasn't having any. But the drinking soon "kind of snowballed" and he began to drink for the express purpose of achieving unconsciousness, or, as he put it, "to get out of reality": "I'd just drink huge amounts of hard liquor just until I could pass out, basically. And it got to the point where I couldn't really drink at all without blacking out and then waking up and finding out I'd done a lot of serious stuff."

When I asked Rick what it was about reality that he was trying to avoid, he told me that growing up he'd always had the nagging sense of being "already in trouble." No matter what he did, he seemed never able to measure up. His parents had little tolerance for anything but the very top performance from him, especially at school, and were routinely punitive and critical if they felt he'd failed them, which was often. On top of that, he was sent to a strict and rather harsh private high school, because his parents felt that the public schools were insufficiently challenging and that Rick needed a strong dose of discipline to live up to his potential. Between the school and his parents, he began to feel that he was "getting it" from all sides: "So by the time I was done with my day of getting punished by my parents and punished by the school, I just wanted to go out and get in trouble."

In high school he "felt stress and tension everywhere, whether it was coming from home, [or] coming from school." There was no one to provide a respite from what he experienced as an unending barrage of criticism:

> At some point I got sick of just having enormous pressure put on me. . . . I realized it was making me severely depressed, and I think that it was probably doing that for a long time. That was one of the key things. It's just I didn't get much support as far as—constructive criticism isn't the right word, but more of like appreciation for what I was doing *right*.

Of his parents he says:

> We're very different actually. We, to this day, still have the same fundamental problems that we've been arguing about since fourth grade. . . . I always had to be doing excellent in school. I mean, I remember in junior high getting in trouble for an A-! So I had a lot of expectations. And my parents went to Harvard, so they were successful. And they both work very hard, [and were] very organized. They're dedicated. And I've always been the opposite of that.

In fact, Rick wasn't the opposite of dedicated and organized: he did very well in school—well enough, in fact, to be admitted to a highly competitive university. But he couldn't escape the feeling that his achievements were never enough in his parents' eyes. It was always, he says, "'Oh, you could have done more work.'"

What particularly got to him was that he did far better in school than most of his friends, whose parents were far more accepting:

> I was in all the AP Honors classes, and every semester I had to take the hardest schedule possible. And my friends were

all in just the normal run-of-the-mill classes. They're, you know, normal—they're at colleges, but the normal colleges. My friends' families would always be . . . telling me that they would love if their kids were doing what I was doing. You know, I was on a sports team. I was doing really well in school. . . . I was pretty much a nice kid, and they were always wondering why I seemed to be getting into big fights with my parents all the time, being grounded all the time. They told me if *their* kids got my grades, they'd be allowed to do whatever they want! A lot of parents, you know, give the kids twenty bucks an A and all that stuff? *My* parents . . . I mean if I got money for *my* grades, I'd be doing *good*.

The sense that they cannot be just normal, without being criticized for not being more, is common among adolescents in the culture of contingent worth. Most parents, to be sure, want to see their children do well. But what distinguishes this strand of American middle-class culture is that the standard of what it means to do well is both unusually high and unusually narrow—and that failing to meet that standard can lead to a totalizing rejection, a fundamental critique of the adolescent's character as a whole. The result is the sense of "constant stress" Rick describes: the inability to ever really relax and simply be yourself, to get outside the struggle for preeminence, to feel confident that you are cared for and appreciated all of the time, rather than just when you win.

"Out There They Accept Anybody"

Rick got past his period of wanting to be "out of reality" by dint of being extremely capable and having, in fact, worked very hard, which allowed him to get into a good college and far enough away from his parents to find his feet and recover his self-respect. Things do not always work out so well. The crushing sense of failure in the face of high and narrow expectations can push middle-class adolescents into seeking out people with different expectations, in what can become a desperate and destructive quest for some kind of success.

CHAPTER 3

Preventing and Treating Teen Addiction

Media-Literate Teens Are Less Susceptible to Addiction

Peter DeBenedittis

According to Peter DeBenedittis, media literacy is a powerful prevention tool that may protect youth against mass media messages that promote destructive values and exacerbate such risky behaviors as underage drinking and drug abuse. DeBenedittis describes media literacy as the ability to critically evaluate television, advertising, and other forms of mass media. Once children and teens understand the techniques employed by various media outlets, DeBenedittis claims, they will be less susceptible to the negative messages that promote unhealthy lifestyles. Peter DeBenedittis is the founder of Media Literacy for Prevention, Critical Thinking, and Self-Esteem, an organization that promotes media literacy education in classrooms throughout the nation.

In mid-March, my friend and I sat in the front row of a minor league ballpark in Tucson, Arizona, watching a spring training game between the Diamondbacks and the Rockies. A woman in her early twenties sat next to us. She asked my friend if he liked her shoes, a pair of bright orange suede Adidas with nifty white stripes. He told her they were all right. Even though he affirmed her, she replied, "I know, but at least my socks are Nike."

By age 18 the average child in America has seen 100,000 commercials on TV. Counting logos, signs, promotions, and all the other mass mediums, this figure soars to nearly twenty million. Behind each ad exposure is a simple message that every child internalizes—you're a loser because you don't own this. No advertising tells us we're okay and don't need to buy

Peter DeBenedittis, "Media Literacy: Saving Children from Self-Hate and Destructive Behavior," *EZine*, October 2005. Reproduced by permission.

anything. Advertising tells us we're uncool, missing what's in style, too fat, too bored, or too boring.

Although our political leaders choose to ignore it, over 4,000 scholarly studies have found that *mass media causes societal violence*. The Surgeon General wrote in 1972 that "the debate is over." Recent research has found that higher amounts of television viewing is correlated with underage drinking. Teens that see R-rated movies are three times more likely to drink and smoke. And despite all the blame that alcohol and tobacco companies put on parents they depict as not doing enough in their so-called prevention spots, advertising influences children to smoke twice as much as does peer pressure. The same holds true with alcohol. [J.W.] Grube & [L.] Wallach (1994) found that children who are more aware of beer advertisements have more favorable attitudes toward drinking, and are more likely to report an intention to drink beer once they are adults.

Media literacy is a powerful tool to inoculate youth against the destructive values being sold to them. The National Office on Drug Control Policy (June 2001) reported that "because the(ir) Campaign's entire strategy acknowledges the power and influence of media on America's youth, it is important and appropriate for the initiative to help young people develop their critical thinking skills by further investing in media literacy."

What Is Media Literacy?

Media literacy is the ability to "read" television and mass media. Media literacy education teaches people to *access*, *analyze*, *evaluate*, and *produce* media. Children who understand the motivations and production techniques of media are less likely to adopt the unhealthy attitudes or behaviors that mass media depict.

What makes media literacy a powerful prevention tool is that it takes children's natural tendency to rebel, and redirects it towards those selling them addictive lifestyles. Media education represents a new and exciting approach to protecting youth from the unhealthy effects of media—an approach that is not dependent on Hollywood's or Madison Avenue's willingness to accept responsibility for its programming and advertising.

In conversations with some of the 50,000 students I give presentations to each year, I continually hear about the impact media literacy education can have. I've had young girls break into tears after seeing me show how actresses and models are computer enhanced in such ridiculously fake ways. I've gotten letters from ex-smokers expressing their gratitude for saving their lives by showing how tobacco ads can manipulate teens into addiction. The impact of media literacy on prevention is more than anecdotal. Post-tests from tobacco prevention talks I gave show that a third of teen smokers attending make an immediate attempt to quit their habit.

At the 2000 Alcohol Policy XII Conference, I presented the results of a study that found a single 45-minute presentation deconstructing alcohol advertising led to significant changes in the social expectancies middle school students had about drinking. Several peer reviewed studies have been published that found similar results with children as young as the third grade. While at Washington State University, [professor of communications] Erica Austin (1997) published two studies showing a change in children's intention to drink alcohol after a media education program. Participating students were less likely to rate alcohol ads positively, were less attracted to alcohol promotional material, and showed greater disdain for alcohol commercials.

As with alcohol prevention, researchers are beginning to find that media literacy is an effective tool in helping prevent and treat eating disorders. [S.M.] Stormer & [J.K.] Thompson (1995) found that very brief instruction in media literacy given to women in college produced significant pre-to-post program reductions in appearance- and weight-related anxiety. The students were less likely to idealize the slenderness embodied by fashion models and actresses. [L.] Irving, [J.] DuPen, & [S.] Berel (1998) found that high school girls viewing a media literacy film on body image and discussing it reported less internalization of a "thin" beauty standard and lower perceived realism of media images than did their comparison group.

Media literacy education can also reduce children's susceptibility to violence. A study conducted with English 8- and 9-year-olds demonstrated changes in children's comprehension and awareness of media violence. In 1983, [L. Rowell] Huesmann, *et. al.*, found statistically significant changes in children's attitudes about media violence using media literacy. Their treatment simply consisted of two training sessions within a 2-week period where third graders wrote essays for a video about how harmful television violence can be.

The Role of Teachers and Parents

Parents and teachers can take back control of the values being taught to our children. It doesn't take a lot of effort, either, to teach a child to be media literate. One study found that parents who talk back to their TV sets had children who were less likely to drink in their teens. The American Academy of Pediatrics has a wonderful website with tips for teachers and parents called Media Matters.

The beauty of teaching media literacy for prevention is that students love learning about media. Schools also embrace media literacy because, ultimately, students are being taught critical thinking skills. And if these are not reasons enough, the preventive value of media literacy is not substance or behavior specific. The media literacy skills used to deconstruct and build resistance to tobacco advertising are the same ones used to prevent underage drinking, violence, eating disorders and other risky behaviors. I encourage you to become a cultural revolutionary and begin to learn and promote media literacy.

For more information, visit www.medialiteracy.net.

Traditional Anti-Drug Programs Are Ineffective

Renee Moilanen

Today's anti-drug programs claim to have replaced what many believe to be the ineffective sloganeering and scare tactics exemplified by the anti-drug curricula of the 1980s, most prominently Drug Abuse Resistance Education (DARE). Renee Moilanen argues, however, that the new drug education programs are based on the same flawed rhetoric meant to scare kids off drugs—and are equally ineffective. A more meaningful approach, according to Moilanen, might abandon the traditional abstinence-only message and instead inculcate an ethic of moderation by giving adolescents the factual information they need to stay safe, even if they choose to experiment. Moilanen is a freelance journalist.

That three-word mantra "Just Say No" became a national punch line for a reason: It didn't keep kids away from drugs. Drug use among teenagers dropped steadily from the early 1980s until 1992, mirroring a decline in drug use among adults. But this downward trend began before the anti-drug curricula developed in the 1980s, exemplified by Drug Abuse Resistance Education (DARE), could have had any impact. The drop was detected in surveys of students who had never heard of DARE or Just Say No. And by the early 1990s, when students who were exposed to DARE and similar programs in grade school and middle school reached their late teens, drug use among teenagers was going up again. In the 2002 Monitoring the Future Study, 53 percent of high school seniors said they had used illegal drugs, compared to 41 percent in 1992. Past-month use rose from 14 percent to 25 percent during the same period.

Meanwhile, the leading model for drug education in the United States has been DARE, which brings police officers into elementary and middle school classrooms to warn kids away from drugs. DARE claims to teach kids how to resist peer pressure and say no to drugs through skits, cartoons, and hypothetical situations. Founded by Los Angeles Police Chief Daryl Gates in 1983 and organized as a nonprofit corporation (DARE America) in 1987, DARE is still used in around three-quarters of the nation's school districts. At the annual DARE Officers Association Dinner a few years ago, Bill Clinton's drug czar, Barry McCaffrey, declared that "DARE knows what needs to be done to reduce drug use among children, and you are doing it—successfully." But as McCaffrey should have known, the effectiveness of DARE has never been demonstrated, a fact DARE America itself implicitly conceded when it announced, half a year after the drug czar's praise, that it was revamping its program.

DARE Is Ineffective

[Since the 1990s] DARE has been widely criticized as unproven and unsophisticated. In one of the most damning studies, published in 1999, a team of researchers at the University of Kentucky found that 10 years after receiving the anti-drug lessons, former DARE students were no different from non-DARE students in terms of drug use, drug attitudes, or self-esteem. "This report adds to the accumulating literature on DARE's lack of efficacy in preventing or reducing substance use," the researchers noted. In a 2003 report, the [U.S.] General Accounting Office reviewed six long-term evaluations of DARE and concluded that there were "no significant differences in illicit drug use between students who received DARE ... and students who did not." The surgeon general, the National Academy of Sciences, and the U.S. Department of Education also have declared DARE ineffective.

Determined not to repeat past mistakes and prodded by a federal government that lately has been demanding accountability in education, teachers today are turning to prevention programs backed by "scientifically based" claims of effectiveness. In 1998 the Department of Education, concerned that money was being wasted on a mishmash of ineffective programs, decided to fund only those proven by "scientifically based research" to reduce or prevent drug use. Testimonials and we-think-it's-working assurances like those cited by DARE would no longer pass muster. Every prevention program now needed hard numbers, objective experiments, and independently reviewed conclusions based on long-term follow-ups to prove they worked.

In 2000 the Department of Education convened an expert panel that judged nine prevention programs "exemplary" for their proven effectiveness and 33 others "promising." Comprised mostly of educators and health professionals, the panel gave the "exemplary" or "promising" nod only to programs backed by at least one scientific evaluation of effectiveness (DARE did not make the cut). Schools using programs that were not on the list would risk losing their slice of the Department of Education's $635 million drug prevention budget. In 2001 President George W. Bush included the "scientifically based research" criterion for drug education in his No Child Left Behind Act, signing into law what had previously been only administrative practice.

But the officially endorsed alternatives to DARE aren't necessarily better. Once you remove the shiny packaging and discard the "new and improved" labels, you'll find a product that's disappointingly familiar. The main thing that has changed is the rhetoric. Instead of "Just Say No," you'll hear, "Use your refusal skills." The new programs encourage teachers to go beyond telling kids that drug use is bad. Instead, they tell teenagers to "use your decision making skills" to make "healthy life choices." Since drugs aren't healthy, the choice is obvious: Just say no.

The persistence of this theme is no accident. Prevention programs can get the federal government's stamp of approval only if they deliver "a clear and consistent message that the illegal use of drugs" is "wrong and harmful." But this abstinence-only message leaves teenagers ill-equipped to avoid drug-related hazards if they do decide to experiment.

After examining some of the new anti-drug curricula and watching a sampling of them in action, I strongly doubt these programs are winning many hearts and minds. . . .

The Kids Know Better

What all of these programs continue to ignore is the most crucial piece in the drug prevention puzzle—the kids, and their stubbornly independent reactions to propaganda. They aren't fooled by "decision making" skills or "healthy choices." They know what the teachers expect: Just say no.

"They make you feel as bad as they can if you do it," says one Los Angeles teenager. Still, he says, "almost every person I know has tried marijuana. Even good people."

At Mira Costa High School in Manhattan Beach, California, a 10th-grade summer health teacher, Guy Gardner, recognizes his difficult position. About one in four Manhattan Beach students are "current" (past-month) marijuana users, according to the district's own studies, which puts them near the national average. "A lot of them know more than I do," Gardner confesses. Yet he plays the game, rattling off a list of warnings—cocaine will rot out your nose, marijuana could kill you, there's no such thing as recreational drug use—even as most of his students know how unlikely or just plain wrong it all is.

In one lesson, Gardner asks students to name the first thing that comes to their minds when they hear the word *drugs.* "Don't give me answers I want to hear, give me your answers," he urges.

A couple of kids call out: Crime. Death. Stupid. Something that alters your mind and screws up your body.

But a few offer another point of view.

"I think it's bad, but people have the choice to do it, and if they do it, it's their problem," says one boy.

"If you really want to do it, you're going to do it," says another, even going so far as to advocate legalizing drugs. "We'd be so much more chill in the nation."

That may be, but saying so is untenable in the abstinence-only world of drug education. Gardner pulls back the debate. You can't legalize drugs, he tells the students, because they're harmful. "The ultimate message" of legalization, he says, "is it's OK to do drugs." And that, he implies, just isn't true.

A New Approach to Drug Education

In the end, meaningful drug education reform probably won't come from educators. It will have to come from those who have far more at stake when it comes to drug use by teenagers: their parents. They are the ones who see their kids stumble home with bloodshot eyes, who can't fall asleep when their kids are partying the night away, who know their kids are experimenting with drugs and want, above all, for them to be safe.

That's why drug experts such as *Safety First* author Marsha Rosenbaum are calling for a truly new approach to drug education, one that abandons the abstinence-only message and gives kids the unbiased, factual information they need to stay safe, even if they choose to experiment. Such information could include now-forbidden advice on real but avoidable hazards such as driving under the influence, having sex when you're high, mixing alcohol with other depressants, and overheating while using Ecstasy.

One possible model is Mothers Against Drunk Driving (MADD), which recognized that if it couldn't stop young people from drinking, it could at least stop them from getting behind the wheel while intoxicated. MADD's efforts, which made *designated driver* a household term, seem to have worked: Since 1982, according to the National Highway Traffic Safety Administration, the number of teenagers killed in drunk driving accidents has plunged 57 percent. MADD thus helped prove that we can make drug use safer without eliminating it entirely.

"There are kids who are not going to use drugs for religious reasons, because they're athletes, because they're focused on school, because they don't like the way they feel," Rosenbaum notes. "These kids don't need a program to tell them no. They're already not using. But for the kids who are amenable to the experience, it doesn't matter how many DARE programs they sit through; they're going to do it anyway. . . . If we can't prevent drug use, what we can prevent is drug abuse and drug problems. But we have to get real."

An Overview of Adolescent Drug Treatment Programs

Timmen L. Cermak

Many options are available to treat not only drug addiction, but also the behavioral and emotional problems that are caused or exacerbated by drug abuse. In the following selection, Timmen Cermak outlines an array of popular drug treatment plans, including education and counseling. At the same time, Cermak addresses the unique problems associated with adolescent drug addiction; psychological maturation and other crucial developmental tasks, for example, are often delayed in adolescents who exhibit addictive behaviors. The following is excerpted from Cermak's book Marijuana: What's a Parent to Believe?

Almost every inpatient treatment program for adolescent chemical dependence is based on what has come to be known as the Minnesota Model, although there are differences in emphasis at different centers. The Minnesota Model emerged in the alcohol field as treatment freed itself from traditional psychiatric medical models that had never proved very helpful. The new idea was a radical departure from Freudian notions of why people became alcoholic. Rather than look for root causes to treat, the Minnesota Model accepted AA's [Alcoholics Anonymous's] notion that alcoholism is a primary disease, similar to an allergy. From this perspective, treatment focuses on establishing and maintaining abstinence rather than trying to uncover and analyze underlying psychological causes for drinking. Treatment introduces patients to the Twelve Steps [of AA] through a series of structured assignments and lectures. Psychotherapy and cognitive-behavioral approaches are directed toward removing whatever psycho-

Timmen L. Cermak, from *Marijuana: What's a Parent to Believe?* Center City, MN: Hazelden, 2003, pp. 167–77. © 2003 by Hazelden Foundation. All rights reserved. Reprinted by permission of Hazelden Foundation.

logical barriers people have to working these Steps and identifying with the recovering community. In short, treatment supplements the Twelve Step approach with an eye toward eventually enabling patients to remain sober with the support of Twelve Step programs.

On the other hand, some outpatient programs exist today that approach alcoholism very differently—as a bad habit, not a disease. They reject the idea that total abstinence is necessary and offer techniques to teach people controlled drinking. Similarly, some outpatient programs treating drug abuse are guided by a philosophy of harm reduction, which helps people reduce their drug use or switch to the use of less harmful drugs. These two approaches rely more heavily on the use of cognitive-behavioral treatment techniques, using education to change how people think about alcohol and other drug use in order to alter their behavior. They offer an alternative to treatment approaches based on Twelve Step principles.

Nearly all inpatient and the bulk of outpatient treatment programs, however, are either directly based on the Twelve Steps or are careful to remain consistent with this philosophy. Residential programs exist on a continuum ranging from social model centers that rely almost exclusively on introducing patients to Twelve Step programs to medical centers that specialize in what have become known as co-occurring disorder patients—chemical dependents who also suffer from co-occurring psychiatric conditions such as depression, major anxiety, or bipolar disorder.

Because there are variations in emphasis from one treatment center to the next, it is difficult to provide generalizations about the residential treatment that is available for adolescents with marijuana dependence. In most adolescent treatment centers, Twelve Step approaches will play a prominent role. As a result, treatment can be expected to be based on the following principles.

Total Abstinence from Addictive Drugs

Total abstinence from addictive drugs is a mainstay for most treatment programs. People who try to abstain from one drug while using other drugs have not broken the core process of addiction. They are still using chemicals to avoid dealing with emotions. They continue to diminish, rather than nurture, awareness in response to distress. Recovery requires a deep commitment and an unbending intention to stay present and aware.

The scientific basis for encouraging abstinence from *all* drugs of abuse lies within the reward center [of the brain]. All addictive drugs eventually lead to an increase in the brain chemical dopamine within the reward center. Any drug that increases dopamine levels keeps the gateway toward addiction open and well greased. As a result, any drug of abuse can trigger euphoric recall of an addict's original drug of addiction and lead to relapse. Substituting alcohol for marijuana, or marijuana for opiates or cocaine, keeps the reward center from returning to its normal baseline as much as it is able.

Education

Education is a standard part of treatment—education about drugs and how they affect the body and brain, emotions, relationships, and spiritual life. Education about healthy psychological tools for coping with stress is also necessary. Unless people in recovery are able to recognize stress and other triggers for their pot use, relapse becomes likely. Relapse prevention is a critical part of all treatment programs and requires multiple skills, including recognition of emotional states and external triggers for relapse, assertiveness training to resist peer pressure, and cognitive-behavioral skills to convert impulses to use drugs into red flags signaling stress.

Process Groups

Process groups are key to helping people early in abstinence to begin dealing with the continual ebb and flow of emotional energy. Therapy groups operate on two important assumptions. First, shared pain becomes lighter. Living openly and publicly among other recovering people promotes healthy habits. If we are as sick as our secrets, then learning to live openly and vulnerably is the antidote. Second, the power of the group often enables individuals to attempt and accomplish things they could never do alone. Recovery happens in community. Process groups provide the healthiest communities many addicts have ever known, certainly healthier than any they have experienced for quite some time.

Stress Busters

Stress busters are an important part of what has to be learned and practiced in treatment programs. Good nutrition, exercise, sufficient sleep, proper hygiene, and a regular schedule are all part of teaching people how to cope better with stress. In addition, many programs routinely teach stress-reduction techniques such as meditation and yoga, which contribute to maintaining a balanced life. For many adolescents, the discipline of self-care will need to be learned for the first time, which often requires a behaviorally-oriented approach.

Respect, Love, and Hope

Respect, love, and hope are all qualities that treatment programs attempt to wrap around addicts as they gradually emerge from their drug-induced fog. Despite its many flaws, the world is still a beautiful place. Human beings can be the source of much pain to each other, but they can also be benevolent beyond belief. Treatment programs frequently hire addicts and alcoholics with several years of recovery to work closely with patients. Not only do they provide solid role models, but they also respond compassionately to people awakening to the miracle of recovery. The respect, love, and hope they have learned to feel toward themselves flood outward to anyone who is earnestly striving to free himself or herself from addiction.

Recovery

Finally, as previously outlined, treatment programs work to successfully introduce people in early abstinence to recovery. Put succinctly, recovery entails a commitment to achieve more than abstinence. With abstinence alone, people never repair the wreckage of the past that addiction leaves in its wake. This is particularly devastating to adolescents, because this wreckage includes disruptions of their psychological development toward adulthood. Whenever people accept the need for recovery, they are acknowledging the need for fundamental changes if they are ever to live full, rich, and satisfying lives without the aid of drugs and alcohol. The "work" of recovery involves learning a set of tools and practicing their use throughout every day. The slogans ("One day at a time," "First things first," etc.), working with a sponsor, service to others, reading, and meditation need to be incorporated into daily life for recovery to become a reality.

Of course, with adolescents there is no fully developed personality to "recover" once abstinence has been achieved. For them, recovery includes working on the process of maturation.

Family Involvement

Family involvement during a child's residential treatment is extremely important if the teen is going to receive the most effective treatment for addiction. This is a time of immense change for the adolescent, and the family often has to change to accommodate the new demands of recovery. In most cases this entails a visit to the treatment center by parents and siblings, although each family's involvement needs to be individualized (for example, in some cases grandparents will also be included; in other cases not all siblings will be included). . . .

Active Intervention

Active intervention is more frequently required with addicted adolescents because emotional and psychological damage accumulates so much more rapidly during adolescence than during adulthood. If an adult takes five years to gather enough evidence that he or she is being hurt by marijuana use, this is *time* lost, personally and professionally. But if a teen takes five years, basically his or her entire adolescent *development* has been lost. It is far harder to recover from missed development as a teen than it is from missed opportunities as an adult. Without the active participation, and often the initiative, of parents, treatment is far less likely to happen.

Separation from the Using Environment

Separation from the using environment is a standard facet of treatment for both adults and adolescents. A difference often exists, however, between an adult's work environment and a teen's school environment. Many adults can receive adequate treatment while still working because their social network of other drinkers and users is an evening and weekend phenomenon. Intensive outpatient treatment programs that meet evenings and help to structure weekends are often sufficient to separate someone from his or her using friends. Such separation can be more difficult for teens, because the school environment is often where they hang out with other users, buying, selling, and using drugs throughout the day. For this reason, residential treatment that temporarily removes teens completely from their usual environment is frequently warranted and often required.

In a similar vein, many teens find it useful to transfer to smaller charter schools specifically designed to support recovery. For teens, social relationships are intense and generally not balanced by concerns that adults might have (e.g., starting a family or professional development). Helping teens establish relationships with healthy and recovering peers puts them in a strong position to resist any temptation that pulls them back toward their old environments. As a result, residential treatment often requires significant decisions regarding school placement as part of the adolescent's discharge planning which may necessitate more than the thirty days initially allotted by many insurance plans.

Underlying Issues and Other Psychiatric Problems

Underlying issues and other psychiatric problems such as depression, eating disorders, untreated ADD [attention deficit disorder], or trauma-induced symptoms need to be addressed up front when treating adolescent addiction. When psychiatric conditions have been "self-medicated" by marijuana, it is important to provide effective relief early in abstinence. Medical treatment requires delicate handling. It can confuse a teen who is finally trying to face life without the aid of any chemicals to be given pills to help with facing life.

When adults want to talk a lot about past traumas too early in recovery, they can get distracted from fully accepting their chemical dependence. But the past is not remote for adolescents; childhood is still upon them. Many find that feelings about their parents' divorce, death, abusive behavior, or alcohol or drug addiction—feelings that they submerged with pot—start resurfacing with abstinence. These feelings need to be addressed head-on if teens are ever going to trust that parents are truly concerned with the world as they experience it. Skilled chemical dependence treatment counselors facilitate a recovering teen's reconnection to these buried feelings, treating them as valid and increasing the teen's awareness of how using pot kept them suppressed. Recovery is a time to calculate the cost of using drugs to manipulate one's emotional life.

Developmental Tasks

Developmental tasks that have been aborted by an adolescent's addiction need to be addressed from the very onset of abstinence. In early recovery, most teens feel grossly out of sync with their peers. Emotional maturation is neglected while using, leading teens early in recovery to feel both young and old at the same time, young because they lag behind their peers in emotional and psychological development and old because they have often lost much of the innocence of others their age who have avoided addiction. Teens in early recovery often feel strangely inept without their drug. They may feel too anxious to speak up to a teacher or easily overwhelmed by whatever emotions spring up within them. The only identity they have is that of a loner and that suddenly is no longer who they are. Rather than finding themselves far ahead of their peers, as they had imagined themselves when using, they now experience themselves as lagging behind, clueless as to how to navigate through the real world successfully. Unless they are quickly guided through neglected developmental tasks, adolescents in early recovery can easily be overwhelmed. To prevent relapse, they need to learn how to accept responsibility for their lives as quickly as possible. The treatment milieu immediately begins the process of holding adolescents accountable for their behavior. An important reason for involving families in treatment is to help parents continue setting the same limits and enforcing the same consequences that their teen responded to in the treatment environment.

Group Therapy

Group therapy is needed to give adolescents an opportunity to connect with peers who are in the same challenging situation. No amount of contact with wise and helpful adults can ever substitute for the value of being with other adolescents in recovery. Discovering that peers have experienced the same doubts and struggles and have the same hopes and longings validates adolescents in ways that no adult ever can. Group therapy provides the arena where adolescents in recovery begin working out the mechanics of healthier relationships.

Structured Environments

Structured environments embody recovery for adolescents. Unlike adults who discontinue using alcohol and other drugs, adolescents can never be exposed to peers with long-term recovery under their belt. By the time teens have several years of successful recovery, they are no longer adolescents. As a result, treatment programs must rely on structured milieus to contain adolescents, all of whom are relatively early in recovery. The structure in residential settings may include prohibiting contact with family except for supervised phone calls in order to decrease the opportunities for pleading to come home and increase a teen's acceptance that he or she is in treatment for the long haul. It may include no contact by phone, mail, or e-mail with friends outside treatment. There is usually a dress code, especially geared to prevent drug-associated messages from contaminating the treatment environment. Little free time is provided, as treatment is not a time for socializing but for serious work. A lot of physical exercise may be part of the structure to provide useful outlets for excess energy as well as to improve physical conditioning, with its positive effect on mood. Many treatment programs are found in remote locations, which decreases the number of runaways without having to resort to locked doors or fences.

Student Drug Testing Reduces Teen Addiction

Office of National Drug Control Policy

Few would question the premise that a drug-free school environment would benefit children and adolescents. The question of how best to address the problem of illicit drug use in the nation's schools, however, generates considerable debate. One proposed solution is student drug testing. Indeed, many parents and school officials endorse school-based drug testing, not as a stand-alone response to the problem, but as a valuable component in the fight to prevent or reduce student drug use. In the following viewpoint, the Office of National Drug Control Policy, a federal agency formed in 1988 to establish policies to support the nation's antidrug program, states its position that student drug testing would not only deter the initiation of drug use, but also identify adolescents who need treatment.

Thanks to advances in medical technology, researchers are now able to capture pictures of the human brain under the influence of drugs. As these images clearly show, the pleasurable sensations produced by some drugs are due to actual physical changes in the brain. Many of these changes are long-lasting, and some are irreversible. Scientists have recently discovered that the brain is not fully developed in early childhood, as was once believed, but is in fact still growing even in adolescence. Introducing chemical changes in the brain through the use of illegal drugs can therefore have far more serious adverse effects on adolescents than on adults.

Even so-called soft drugs can take a heavy toll. Marijuana's effects, for example, are not confined to the "high"; the drug can also cause serious problems with memory and learning, as

Office of National Drug Control Policy, "Drug Testing: An Overview," September 20, 2002. www.whitehousedrugpolicy.gov.

well as difficulty in thinking and problem solving. Use of methamphetamine or Ecstasy (MDMA) may cause long-lasting damage to brain areas that are critical for thought and memory. In animal studies, researchers found that four days of exposure to Ecstasy caused damage that persisted for as long as six or seven years. Kids on drugs cannot perform as well in school as [do] their drug-free peers of equal ability. So if testing reduces students' use of illicit drugs, it will remove a significant barrier to academic achievement.

A Reward for Staying Clean

In rural Autauga County, Alabama, students have a special incentive to stay off drugs. As part of a voluntary drug-testing program, participating students who test negative for drugs in random screenings receive discounts and other perks from scores of area businesses.

Community leaders and school officials, prompted by a growing concern about the use of drugs, alcohol, and cigarettes among students, launched the program in 2000 with the help of a local drug-free coalition called Peers Are Staying Straight (PASS). "Our community was awakening to the fact that we needed to do something," says PASS Executive Director Martha Ellis.

The Independent Decision program began with just the 7th grade but will expand each year to include all grade levels. In the 2001–2002 school year, more than half of all 7th and 8th graders at public and private schools participated.

To enter the program, kids take a urine test for nicotine, cocaine, amphetamines, opiates, PCP, and marijuana. Those who test negative get a picture ID that entitles them to special deals at more than 55 participating restaurants and stores. Students keep the ID as long as they test negative in twice-yearly random drug tests.

Those who test positive (there have been only three) must relinquish their cards and any special privileges. The school counselor notifies the parents and, if appropriate, offers advice about where to find help. At that point, the matter is strictly in the parents' hands. If the child tests negative in a subsequent random test, his or her card is returned. "Our whole purpose," says Ellis, "is to reward kids who stay clean and help them see the benefits of a drug-free lifestyle."

Surveys taken by PRIDE (the National Parents' Resource Institute for Drug Education) before the program began and again in 2002 showed significant reductions in drug use among Autauga County's 8th graders: from 35.9 percent to 24.4 percent for nicotine, 39.9 percent to 30 percent for alcohol, and 18.5 percent to 11.8 percent for marijuana. . . .

Preventing Use and Abuse

Substance abuse should be recognized for what it is–a major health issue—and dealt with accordingly. Like vision and hearing tests, drug testing can alert parents to potential problems that continued drug use might cause, such as liver or lung damage, memory impairment, addiction, overdose, even death. Once the drug problem has been identified, intervention and then treatment, if appropriate, can begin.

Testing can also be an effective way to prevent drug use. The expectation that they may be randomly tested is enough to make some students stop using drugs—or never start in the first place.

That kind of deterrence has been demonstrated many times over in the American workplace. Employees in many national security and safety-sensitive positions—airline pilots, commercial truck drivers, school bus drivers, to name a few—are subject to pre-employment and random drug tests to ensure public safety. Employers who have followed the Federal model have seen a 67-percent drop in positive drug tests. Along with significant declines in absenteeism, accidents, and healthcare costs, they've also experienced dramatic increases in worker productivity.

While some students resist the idea of drug testing, many endorse it. For one thing, it gives them a good excuse to say "no" to drugs. Peer pressure among young people can be a powerful and persuasive force. Knowing they may have to submit to a drug test can help kids overcome the pressure to take drugs by giving them a convenient "out." This could serve them well in years to come: Students represent the workforce of tomorrow, and eventually many will need to pass a drug test to get a job.

It is important to understand that the goal of school-based drug testing is not to punish students who use drugs. Although consequences for illegal drug use should be part of any testing program—suspension from an athletic activity or revoked parking privileges, for example—the primary purpose is to deter use and guide those who test positive into counseling or treatment. In addition, drug testing in schools should never be undertaken as a stand-alone response to the drug problem. Rather, it should be one component of a broader program designed to reduce students' use of illegal drugs.

What Are the Benefits of Drug Testing?

Drug use can quickly turn to dependence and addiction, trapping users in a vicious cycle that destroys families and ruins lives. Students who use drugs or alcohol are statistically more likely to drop out of school than their peers who don't. Dropouts, in turn, are more likely to be unemployed, to depend on the welfare system, and to commit crimes. If drug testing deters drug use, everyone benefits—students, their families, their schools, and their communities.

Drug and alcohol abuse not only interferes with a student's ability to learn, it also disrupts the orderly environment necessary for all students to succeed. Studies have shown that students who use drugs are more likely to bring guns and knives to school, and that the more marijuana a student smokes, the greater the chances he or she will be involved in physical attacks, property destruction, stealing, and cutting classes. Just as parents and students can expect schools to offer protection from violence, racism, and other forms of abuse, so do they have the right to expect a learning environment free from the influence of illegal drugs.

What Are the Risks?

Schools should proceed with caution before testing students for drugs. Screenings are not 100 percent accurate, so every positive screen should be followed by a laboratory-based confirming test. Before going ahead with tests, schools should also have a good idea of precisely what drugs their students are using. Testing for just one set of illegal drugs when others pose an equal or greater threat would do little to address a school's drug problem.

Confidentiality is a major concern with students and their parents. Schools have a responsibility to respect students' privacy, so it is vital that only the people who need to know the test results see them—parents and school administrators, for example. The results should not be shared with anyone else, not even teachers.

Student Drug Testing Is Invasive and Counterproductive

Janice M. Eisen

Janice M. Eisen is opposed to random student drug testing on several counts. First, according to Eisen, drug tests violate the privacy rights of teens. In addition, drug testing, in Eisen's view, has little, if any, impact on student drug use. Perhaps more importantly, Eisen writes, drug testing may be counterproductive: The threat of a drug test may discourage teens from participating in extracurricular activities that keep them busy, supervised—and away from the temptation to use drugs. Eisen is a freelance writer and editor.

Pewaukee High School announced [in mid-2005] that the first year of its drug-testing program had yielded three positive results for drugs. Several other school districts have expressed interest in implementing similar plans.

I hope they will reconsider and that the Pewaukee School District, despite its three "successes," will think about ending its program.

Few, if any, would question the aim of reducing the use of drugs, or alcohol and tobacco, by adolescents. What I question is random, suspicionless drug testing as a means of doing so.

In 2002, the U.S. Supreme Court ruled that school districts may conduct drug tests of students who participate in extracurricular activities without probable cause; that is, without any reason to suspect the student is using drugs. Most adults would balk at being randomly ordered to urinate within sound or sight of a monitor. However, teenagers' privacy apparently is not valued.

Janice M. Eisen, "Student Drug Testing Is Not the Answer," *Milwaukee Journal Sentinel*, July 7, 2005. Reproduced by permission of the author.

A drug-testing program is likely to produce two different reactions among those tested: increased resentment of authority or, worse, sheeplike compliance after hearing the rote phrase, "If you have nothing to hide, why should it bother you?" That is a frightening attitude to instill in our future citizens unless we are preparing them to live in a police state.

Like most people, a Supreme Court majority felt that stopping teen drug use overrides civil liberties concerns. Here's a more convincing reason to avoid random drug testing: It doesn't work. In fact, it is probably counterproductive.

In 2003, researchers partly funded by the government's National Institute on Drug Abuse published the first large-scale study of the effects of school drug testing. They found that it had no impact on student drug use.

But ineffectiveness is not why groups including the American Academy of Pediatrics, the American Public Health Association and the National Council on Alcoholism and Drug Dependence signed a friend-of-the-court brief in the 2002 case.

They felt compelled, in the words of the brief, "to resist measures, however well-intentioned, that are inconsistent with" the objective of preventing teenage drug abuse in other words, because drug testing can be counterproductive.

Extracurricular Activities and Drug Testing

Studies have shown what common sense suggests: Teens participating in athletics or extracurricular activities are a relatively low-risk group for drug use. Pewaukee High could be examining the urine of Chess Club and Pep Squad members when the students in real danger are hanging around the parking lot.

The most obvious way extracurricular participation protects students is by keeping them busy and supervised. The period between the end of the school day and parents' arrival home is the most dangerous time for teens, when a disproportionate amount of dangerous behavior, including drug use, happens.

That's not the only way extracurricular activities help keep students away from drugs. Those who participate get social support from other motivated students and from faculty they get to know outside the classroom.

What might happen when schools institute a drug-testing requirement for participation in after-school activities? Some students will refuse to participate in the activities, and those most likely to skip it are precisely the ones activities would help most the kids on the margins who aren't already involved and motivated. Those with something to hide will avoid the very programs.

If drug testing worked, it might be worth the privacy loss and the cost ($1,000 per positive result in Pewaukee). But research shows it fails to reduce student drug use, and experts in child health and substance abuse believe it does harm.

There are effective education, prevention and treatment programs out there. We should demand our schools find them, instead of wasting money on the appearance of doing something about drug use.

Stronger Public Policies Are Needed to Prevent Marijuana Addiction

Joseph A. Califano Jr.

Joseph A. Califano Jr. is president of the National Center on Addiction and Substance Abuse at Columbia University. In the following viewpoint Califano cites research findings that suggest that adolescent marijuana use presents significant social and health issues. To Califano, then, reducing marijuana use "makes eminent sense." To this end, Califano advocates a variety of measures that combine public policy with law enforcement—requiring teens arrested for marijuana possession to participate in educational classes and programs geared to discourage and treat marijuana abuse, for example.

The increased potency of today's marijuana and the greater knowledge we have of the dangers of using marijuana justify the increased attention that law enforcement is giving to illegal possession of the drug. But the disappointing reality is that a nearly 30 percent increase in marijuana arrests does not translate into a comparable reduction in use of the drug. Something more is needed.

[Former mayor] Rudolph Giuliani's success in slashing New York City's crime rate by, among other things, going after low-level street crimes such as smoking and selling small amounts of marijuana inspired many other mayors to follow suit. When President [George W.] Bush announced in 2002 a goal of reducing illegal drug use by 10 percent in two years and 25 percent in five years, he knew he had to focus on cutting marijuana use. Eliminating all other illegal drug use combined would not even get him close to his highly touted objective.

Joseph A. Califano Jr., "U.S. Must Cut Marijuana Use Among Teens," *Deseret News (Salt Lake City)*, May 22, 2005. Reproduced by permission.

From the standpoint of protecting children, teens and the public health, reducing marijuana use makes eminent sense. For even though marijuana use has leveled off or waned slightly over the past several years, the number of children and teenagers in treatment for marijuana dependence and abuse has jumped 142 percent since 1992, and the number of teen emergency room admissions in which marijuana is implicated is up almost 50 percent since 1999. Though alcohol remains by far the teen substance of choice, teens are three times likelier to be in treatment for marijuana than for alcohol (and six times likelier to be in treatment for marijuana than for all other illegal drugs combined).

The Dangers of Marijuana Use

As has been true of tobacco since the 1900s, we've learned a lot about the dangers of marijuana since the 1970s. The drug adversely affects short-term memory, the ability to concentrate and motor skills. Recent studies indicate that it increases the likelihood of depression, schizophrenia and other serious mental health problems. Nora Volkow, director of the National Institute on Drug Abuse, has repeatedly expressed concern about the adverse impact of marijuana on the brain, a matter of particular moment for youngsters whose brains are still in the development stage. Volkow has stated: "There is no question marijuana can be addictive; that argument is over. The most important thing right now is to understand the vulnerability of young, developing brains to these increased concentrations of cannabis."

The issue of marijuana use (and most illegal drug use) is all about kids. If we can get kids not to smoke marijuana before they reach age 21, they are virtually certain never to do so. So let's do more than trumpet the arrest rate. Let's focus on discouraging children and teens from getting involved with the drug in the first place.

This begins with understanding the importance of preventing kids from becoming cigarette smokers. Most kids who smoke cigarettes will not smoke marijuana, but a 2003 survey of 12- to 17-year-olds, conducted by the National Center on Addiction and Substance Abuse (CASA) at Columbia University, reveals that teens who smoke cigarettes are much likelier than nonsmokers to try marijuana; they are also likelier to become regular marijuana users.

Forging Public Policy

The next question is how to make public policies, including law enforcement approaches, more effective in discouraging marijuana use. Availability is the mother of use, so doing a far better job of reducing availability is high on the list. Beyond that—and recognizing that reducing demand is key to that goal—we should use the increased arrest rate as an opportunity to discourage use.

Years ago, while I was visiting Los Angeles, then-Mayor Dick Riordan told me that in his city kids were arrested an average of nine times for possession of marijuana before anything happened to them. I have since discovered that this situation is common in many American communities. Most kids do not even get a slap on the wrist the first few times they're nabbed for smoking a joint. As a result, we let them sink deeper and deeper into drug use, with its dangers to their physical, mental and emotional development and its risk of addiction.

I am not suggesting that we put kids in jail for smoking pot. But why not treat a teen arrested for marijuana use much the same way we treat a teen arrested for drunk driving? Why not require kids arrested for marijuana possession to attend classes to learn about the dangers of marijuana use and to develop some skills (and the will) to decline the next time they are offered the drug? The incentive to attend such classes would be the threat of the alternative: for the first couple of arrests, loss of a driver's license or a fine stiff enough to hurt; for continued use, a few nights in a local prison. Getting kids to attend sessions designed to discourage their marijuana use would give some practical meaning to increased law enforcement and would bring reductions in drug use more in line with increased arrest rates.

These steps will help, but the fact is that we cannot arrest our way out of the teen marijuana problem when (in a recent CASA survey) 40 percent of 12- to 17-year-olds report that they can buy the drug within a day, and 21 percent say they can buy it within an hour.

Parents are the first line of defense. Parents must understand that the drug available today is far more potent than what they might have smoked in the 1970s. For their children, smoking marijuana is not a harmless rite of passage but rather a dangerous game of Russian roulette.

CONTEMPORARY
ISSUES
COMPANION

CHAPTER 4

Personal Stories of
Addiction and Recovery

Using Drug Tests to Stay Clean

Noah Harpham

In the following narrative, college student Noah Harpham re-counts the circumstances that surrounded his descent into—and eventual recovery from—marijuana dependency. In his own words, Harpham describes how he came to recognize that he was "mentally and emotionally addicted" only after he was arrested for marijuana possession. At this turning point, Harpham writes, drug tests became an integral part of his recovery because they provided a powerful impetus for him to get—and stay—clean.

I first tried smoking pot when I was a sophomore in high school. It was with my stepbrother on what happened to be "International Marijuana Day," April 20. Up until about one week before this date, if somebody told me that I was soon going to try pot and eventually become a habitual smoker, I would have laughed at the absurdity of the statement.

I was very confident and firm in my stance against drugs. I knew they were bad, and that is about all I needed to know to be sure I wasn't ever going to try them. So how did a "Christian" boy with loving, caring parents and a wonderful life evolve into a "pothead"?

It started with alcohol. I got drunk for my first time at a party, and it was a blast. I rank it as one of the most memorable experiences of my life. That same night, I found out for sure that my stepbrother smoked pot (I'd had my suspicions but never asked). I was told that if I thought alcohol was fun, I would think pot was the best thing in the world.

After a few days of struggling about whether or not to try it, I caved in. I told my stepbrother I wanted to try it, and so we got stoned. From that day, I have been mentally and emotionally addicted. Some experts would say I was addicted before I took my first hit.

Smoking pot was something I enjoyed. I thought that when I was stoned I was smarter, more likable, able to play music better, and, perhaps the most interesting thing, I felt closer to God. The fact is I believe all these things are true. People try to tell me that it was just in my head, but I'm certain it wasn't. My dad would tell me that the closeness I felt to God was only the Devil playing tricks on my mind. Some days I think I agree, and some days I wholeheartedly disagree. The key for me is figuring out how to think and feel what it is when I'm stoned—without actually being stoned.

When my parents first discovered I was using pot, they began to drug test me. I was outraged. It felt like an invasion of my privacy. I felt that as long as I continued to get good grades and stayed out of trouble, it was none of their business if I smoked pot occasionally. It was embarrassing to have to be dragged into the doctor's office and given a drug test. The doctor would ask if it was for a job, and I would say, "No, my mom makes me take them." The doctor would then give me a look and ask if I was going to pass.

I would shrug my shoulders because most of the time I honestly didn't know. It was hit and miss because they were random. I passed a few and I failed a few, but I never quit smoking. Somewhere in the back of my mind, I always knew I had a drug problem, but I could make excuses for myself very easily. It wasn't until I hit the bottom, on March 10, 2000, that I began to admit that I had a problem—and that it was hurting not just me but a lot of other people.

I Have Never Felt So Bad

That morning, I had to get up at about 5 a.m. to pick up a friend on my way to school. We had a very important once-a-year jazz band competition that day at another school located three hours away. The friend I picked up plays guitar and I play bass. When I picked him up, he told me he had some pot. So we smoked a lot of pot before we got to the school and got on the school bus with the other jazz band members. Our jazz band was supposed to play right after lunch. My friend and I thought it would be a good idea to go smoke more pot at lunchtime before we played. We went behind a strip mall located across from the high school and were in the middle of smoking a bowl when a woman who worked at one of the stores came to take out the trash. She spotted us and told us we shouldn't be doing that. We said OK and walked over to McDonald's. About five minutes later, some policemen came into McDonald's. They recognized us by this woman's description, and we were arrested for marijuana possession.

They handcuffed us right there and put us in the back of the cop car and drove us across the street to the high school. They then marched us right through the middle of the school in handcuffs up to the principal's office. We waited while they got our band director (my favorite and most respected teacher) to tell him that half the rhythm section of the jazz band had been arrested. He walked into the office, and I will never forget the look on his face. He was in shock; he didn't know what to say. His favorite student had just been arrested. He had no clue at all that I did drugs. Later, I heard stories about him falling on his knees in tears and that he briefly wondered if he should quit teaching. He told my parents he didn't ever expect to feel that brokenhearted unless one of his own kids got into trouble.

My friend and I waited in silence in a small room while our parents drove over three hours to come pick us up. I have never felt so bad as I did that day.

After the jazz band incident, I realized I had a problem and couldn't quit without help. I've since come to realize that because I am an introverted person with a family history of drug abuse, that makes me a setup for addiction.

Forcing Myself to Stay Clean

Only then, when I welcomed the drug tests as a way to force myself to stay clean (I think it's invasion of privacy when done in the workplace or in schools without any prior reason), were they helpful in keeping me clean. It wasn't foolproof though; I failed one a week before I went off to college.

My dad had told me that if I failed a drug test, he wouldn't pay for the college I wanted to go to; I'd be on my own and have to pay my way to a community college. Thankfully, my dad gave me one more chance (I think my parents really wanted me to go to a good college and thought it might help). I'm currently at Chapman University in Orange, Calif. And if I fail to stay clean here in college, I'll be on my own. It's a lot of motivation to stay clean, but I'm still extremely scared that any day I will give in. The good thing is that I haven't seen one sign of dope yet. A lot of these kids know how to have fun without pot, and I'm learning how, too, I hope. I even joined the surfing club.

I always had a saying that "pot doesn't change my beliefs about God." Which is true in a way, but at the same time it's false. It's true in the sense that I still believe in God when I'm on drugs, but it's false because it distorts my perception of who God is and how he wants me (not the drugs) to see him. I think when I smoked pot I became too easy on myself and started molding God to fit me instead of me molding to fit God. Ultimately, this needs to be my motivation to quit, because deep down I know it's not what God has planned for me.

A Teenage Boy's Addiction to Prescription Painkillers

Laura D'Angelo

OxyContin is a prescribed medication containing a powerful narcotic that, when used for legitimate medical reasons and prescribed by a physician, is a strong and efficient treatment for chronic or debilitating pain. With properties similar to heroin, however, OxyContin is becoming a drug of abuse. In the following selection, Laura D'Angelo recounts one teen's painful addiction to OxyContin. Describing the drug's appeal—and how Oxy-Contin almost took hold of his life—the seventeen-year-old teen recalls, "When I had pills, I'd feel like a king." D'Angelo has written many articles on drugs and addiction.

While 17-year-old Ryan Curry slept, visions of OxyContin danced in his head. Ryan was thrilled to see Oxy pills scattered under the bed, until unbearable cravings jarred him awake. Now, he could see that there were no pills. Drenched in cold sweat, Ryan's body convulsed and he began a frantic search for more OxyContin.

Ryan never thought he'd become addicted to OxyContin, a powerful drug that's prescribed for people with severe pain. Like most prescription medications, when OxyContin is used for the medical reasons prescribed and taken in the dosage and form prescribed, it can ease suffering for millions of Americans. When abused, prescription drugs can push people over the edge into addiction, injury, or even death.

"Medications can be dangerous. Prescription drugs need to be taken by people who are under medical supervision," says Jerry Frankenheim, Ph.D., a pharmacologist at the National Institute on Drug Abuse (NIDA). "Drugs that are abused can change the way your brain functions for a very long time."

Laura D'Angelo, "Crushed Dreams," www.scholastic.com. Reprinted by permission of Scholastic, Inc.

OxyContin, whose active ingredient is oxycodone hydro-chloride, was hailed as revolutionary in 1996 when it appeared on the market. Like some other painkillers, oxycodone is an opioid. It works as heroin does, quieting pain messages by slowing the central nervous system. OxyContin is unique in that each pill releases medication over a 12-hour period. When crushed and snorted, however, the drug acts differently. Then, a day's worth of painkiller hits the user's brain at once, upsetting the normal flow of brain chemicals.

Ryan, who lives in Newport, Maine, had smoked marijuana for four years before experimenting with prescription drugs. "Pot didn't have the same kick that it used to," he says. "I was bored, looking for a thrill, and trying to be cool."

Ryan quickly got hooked on oxycodone. "I felt so euphoric—like I could be happy sitting in a trashcan in the dark somewhere," Ryan says. He turned his girlfriend on and together they joined the small number of teens who abuse OxyContin. According to NIDA, 4 percent of high school seniors reported using OxyContin in 2002, along with 3 percent of 10th-graders and 1.3 percent of 8th-graders. Ryan quit college to work for an electrician to earn cash to buy pills. He began to use more and more OxyContin. "When I had pills, I'd feel like a king," he says. Ryan was building a physical tolerance for the drug and needed more to avoid going through withdrawal. "I'd wake up and snort 30 or 40 milligrams of Oxy—not to get high, but to feel normal, not sick." Over the next two years, Ryan went from that first 20-milligram rush to a 240-milligram-a-day habit.

Opioids that are abused can take over the emotional center of the brain called the limbic system. Craving for the drug replaces other cravings for pleasures like food, friends, and achievement. "The drug becomes the most important thing in people's lives," Frankenheim says.

Hitting Bottom

Ryan's mom had pleaded with him to get help, but Ryan denied he was doing drugs. Finally, Ryan hit bottom when his girlfriend left him. He let his mom take him to a drug treatment center.

Ryan has finally kicked his addiction to OxyContin. He has been drug-free for six months. As treatment, he attends weekly counseling sessions, where he deals with intense feelings that were turned off by Oxy. "Drugs short-circuit the brain," Frankenheim explains. "When a person comes off the drug and the brain starts coming back to normal, it can feel like a rebirth."

True, says Ryan, who sometimes feels like a beginner in his own life. "I cry at movies I've seen before. Yesterday, I put a grape in my mouth and spit it out because it tasted more bitter than I remembered." "I feel sad that I lost those years of my life and would give anything to get them back," Ryan says. "But now I have a life other than drugs. I'm taking college classes. I have clean friends and support. . . . I actually feel. . . . That's a big change."

A Teenage Girl Survives Her Addiction to Ecstasy

Nicole Hansen

In the following narrative Nicole Hansen reflects on her life and how she used ecstasy and other drugs to assuage the feelings of loneliness and self-doubt that had plagued her throughout high school. Writes Hansen, "The only time I felt happy . . . was when I was on Ecstasy." Hansen describes how she resolved to get clean only after a nearly lethal drug overdose sent her into a coma. Although Hansen was able to achieve sobriety, she considers herself a lifelong addict.

I never believed something like this would happen to me, but it did—and it happened fast.

I grew up just outside of Salt Lake City with my parents and younger sister in a typical, middle-class suburb. I had friends, but by high school they were few. I didn't play sports, I wasn't a cheerleader or a dancer or even a thug. I was just me—and often that left me feeling very alone. I didn't feel like I fit in anywhere.

Everything changed during the summer when I was 17. The people I knew started going to raves. I distanced myself from that scene because I thought it was weird. Slowly, though, my perception changed. The more people I knew who went to raves, the more I believed it couldn't be that bad.

That October, I decided to go to a party where I knew people would be doing drugs. Everyone seemed to know each other. I have to admit, I was jealous. I felt like an outsider.

Halfway through the night I met a really awesome guy. After talking for a while he offered me Ecstasy. I decided to try it. As I swallowed the pill I thought, there's no way this could be bad.

All the Partying

A half an hour went by and I began to question its power. But then it hit me like a tidal wave. It was incredible: My senses magnified, the lights became more vivid, the music sounded more beautiful, and my new acquaintances felt like best friends. I didn't even know half of their names and yet I felt I loved them. I loved everything that night. So, it was no wonder why I wanted to feel that way again soon.

Before long I started popping Ecstasy every other Saturday night. It was fun going to parties and meeting new people. Soon I was using every Thursday, Friday and Saturday. I wasn't alone either—even the cheerleaders and football players were using the "love drug." And they were buying the drugs from the basketball players and band members who were selling pills right out of their lockers.

All this partying took its toll on me. My body ached from the hours of dancing. My eyes were bloodshot with big, dark circles around them. I was always sick and depressed. I began to hate everything—I hated school, I hated my job and I fought constantly with my family. I thought that I had the worst life. The only time I felt happy anymore was when I was on Ecstasy. Only the drug was never as good as the time before. Now it seemed that even Ecstasy couldn't numb the pain. So, I began to move on to other drugs—cocaine, ketamine and mushrooms. Despite this, I didn't think I had a problem because I was still working and going to school.

But within three months my recklessness caught up with me. I was at a small house party and started drinking from a container of Red Bull—which turned out to be full of GHB (roughly 10 times the amount usually used recreationally). Although I don't remember what happened, the events of the evening were explained to me:

I became unconscious. My body forced itself to throw up several times. My "friends" weren't too alarmed. They just thought I "G'ed-out" (e.g. passed out from taking too much GHB) and that I would sleep it off. Rather than help me, they just stuck me in the bathroom. I was unconscious for hours and nobody checked on me.

Finally, the owner of the house came home and found me passed out on the bathroom floor. He ran out frantically screaming for answers. When he came back to check on me, I wasn't breathing.

As he and another guy carried me to the car, they had to set me down every 10 feet to give me mouth-to-mouth resuscitation. Luckily, the hospital was only four blocks away. They dropped me off without telling anyone who I was.

Fortunately, the doctors recognized my symptoms and immediately went to work. They used paddles to revive me. Each time they had me breathing, I would stop. I flat lined twice. I was in a coma for three hours.

Wake-Up Call

Waking up was one of the most horrible experiences of my life. I awoke in a strange, white room, my ears ringing so loud it was unbearable. Then I began to choke. I tried to reach up and pull out whatever was in my throat, but I couldn't. My arms and legs were tied down and I panicked—I thought I was going to choke to death. The nurses had to calm me down, coercing me to believe that the tube in my mouth was for my benefit—it was allowing me to breathe.

They asked me if I knew where I was, who I was, or what had happened. I shook my head. I knew nothing.

"You overdosed on GHB," a nurse said. I couldn't believe it.

My mom and dad arrived as soon as they could. They found my room in the intensive care unit; the board outside read: "Jane Doe."

This whole experience was a huge wake-up call. While I was using drugs, I thought I'd made some incredible friends. On the night I needed them most, however, my "friends" were not there for me. They just dumped me in the bathroom, not wanting me to disrupt their good time. Only two people came to see me in the hospital. Of course, these people were not true friends. They were there for me as long as it didn't interfere with their life or their fun, or get them in trouble.

When I left the hospital, I tried to get my life back together. It was hard. I'd gone from partying with groups of people every weekend, to sitting home every night by myself, crying. It wasn't easy giving up my addiction, but it seemed nearly impossible to give up the lifestyle, the "friends." Once I stopped using, they wanted nothing to do with me.

My family has been there for me the whole time, wanting to help and always supporting me. Without them I don't know how I would have ever pulled out of it. When I was ready to tell them everything, I made them promise not to say a word until I was finished. It was just as hard facing my parents as facing my problem. They were in shock at some of the things I told them.

I decided to clean up by myself without rehab or counseling. I got myself into it, so I wanted to get myself out. It may not have been the right way, maybe I should have asked for help. But I made the choice to quit, and I am the one who has stayed clean and sober for over 18 months. But without my parents, I may have relapsed.

Recovery

I have recovered, but not fully. Now, a year and a half later, I still struggle with both short- and long-term memory loss. A lot of the time I don't remember what I said right after I say it.

Because of the choices I made I wasn't able to graduate with my class, but did return the following summer to get my GED [general education development, or high school equivalency degree].

For the rest of my life I'll be in recovery—because just one slip can blow everything. The most important thing for me to remember is that despite the mistakes I've made, I am still a good person and have much to give. I stay clean because I wake up every day and promise myself that I won't do drugs that day. Imagining not doing drugs ever again sounds too overwhelming, so I take it a day at a time.

In 2001, I entered the Miss Teen Utah contest. Many of the other candidates told me that I didn't deserve to be there because of my past. It was hard to hear, but I couldn't let other people's perceptions prevent me from bettering myself. It turns out I won—and the feeling was ten times better than any high I had on drugs.

I also had many incredible experiences such as the privilege to run the 2002 Winter Olympic torch through Spokane, Washington, and appear on the Montel Williams show about club drugs.

Now I'm concentrating on reaching my goals. I recently moved to New York City to pursue my love of singing and performing. I even wrote a song about addiction called "Someone Save Me." During the period of time I was into drugs I forgot about my dreams. But now I have some great things lined up. I made it through something as difficult as drugs and addiction; obtaining my dream will be a piece of cake!

I'm also focusing on educating kids about drugs. I speak at elementary, middle schools, high schools, and on college campuses. I want kids and teens to know what can happen when you choose the wrong path. I have seen both sides, lived both lives. Believe me, I now know how lucky I am to be alive.

Losing It All to Compulsive Gambling

Tan Vinh

Dustin Waggoner started gambling in high school. For Waggoner, this seemingly benign form of entertainment quickly turned into a compulsion that was driven, in part, by the thrill of winning large sums of cash—perhaps "a month's paycheck in one night." Although he has stopped gambling, Waggoner concedes that he must remain vigilant against the lure of gambling that is all around—in televised poker tournaments and Internet gambling, for example. Waggoner's story, as told by reporter Tan Vinh, originally appeared in the Seattle Times.

He pulled all-nighters during freshman year at his dorm— hosting poker parties.

He lost thousands of dollars at casinos, even draining a savings account he'd established for his now-2-year-old son.

And despite going to Gamblers Anonymous meetings and promising his father he'd never gamble again, 20-year-old Dustin Waggoner of Puyallup [Washington] drove to Chips Casino in Lakewood, Pierce County, one night and blew the entire $1,500 in his checking account.

"When I see the casino billboards, I think I can make a month's paycheck in one night," said Waggoner, who started gambling heavily two years ago. "And the only way I leave a casino is when I can't get any more money out of the ATM, or the casino closes."

Waggoner says he has stopped gambling again—for good this time, he hopes—though he still sees the lure of gambling all around him: online, on casino billboards and in televised poker tournaments with winnings of up to $1 million.

A Grouping Problem

Gambling officials, researchers and treatment providers say that, for the vast majority of people who go to casinos and cardrooms or engage in other forms of gaming, gambling is but another form of entertainment. But as the state's legalized gambling industry has grown—with net receipts more than tripling in the past 10 years to nearly $1.7 billion—so, too, have concerns about problem gambling.

The state has identified three groups as being particularly vulnerable—older people; Asians and members of other ethnic groups for whom gambling has deep cultural roots; and young people, who tend to be impulsive.

In high schools around the area, counselors and intervention specialists more accustomed to seeing teens who drink too much, use drugs or suffer from anorexia say they're hearing more about problem gamblers—from friends and parents concerned that a student is playing too much poker with friends or on the Internet.

"Teen gambling is huge, huge. At the high schools it's unbelievable," said Bellevue therapist Margaret Ferris, an expert on teen gambling.

"I see it more on the Eastside because they have access to money. A lot of these kids have their own credit cards. It's not until they spend thousands of dollars that parents wonder, 'What is going on?'"

Many school counselors say the phenomenon is driven in part by the increasing visibility of gambling—especially the poker game Texas Hold 'Em. Toys R Us and KB Toys stores sell poker sets and other casino-related games. Many colleges host casino night as a social event for freshmen, and some poker tournaments offer college scholarships.

As a result, more young adults are gambling, and their addiction rate is higher than that of other age groups, several nationwide studies concluded. The University of Pennsylvania found that nearly 13 percent of boys and young men between the ages of 14 and 22 gamble at cards at least once a week.

The nonprofit Washington State Council on Problem Gambling found that 8.4 percent of teens 13 to 18 have a gambling problem. The rate is likely much higher, many school counselors and therapists say, because the survey was completed in 1999, long before the Texas Hold 'Em craze.

An expert on youth gambling, Dan Romer of the University of Pennsylvania's Annenberg Public Policy Center, warns that this fad is more dangerous than others because teens are more prone than adults to addiction. "They are more compulsive risk-takers," said Romer. "It's sensation-seeking, looking for thrills and kicks without thinking about the consequences," [he adds.]. . .

Winning Came Easy

Waggoner said he started playing poker with classmates during his junior year at Tacoma Baptist Schools.

At 18, he enrolled at York College, a private liberal-arts school in Nebraska where, in his dorm, everyone seemed to be into Texas Hold 'Em. He organized some games, winning up to $300 per night.

In the spring of 2004, after his girlfriend became pregnant, he quit college and returned home, moving in with his parents and delivering furniture to help support his infant son. One day he gambled $50 on blackjack at Chips Casino in Lakewood and won $1,900, the most cash he has ever held in his hands. It was easy, and it made him feel rich.

The next day, he called in sick to work and headed back to the casino, winning another $700. On the third night he hit it big again, he said, winning $2,000. "I was making a whole month's paycheck in a day."

After a shopping spree, he lost the remaining $3,000 at blackjack. Unfazed, he figured he could turn $50 into thousands another night. That's when he became a regular at the casino, rushing there on paydays and typically betting $200 a hand.

When his cash ran out, he bet the money for his car payments. One night, he even withdrew the $1,000 from an account he'd set up for his son and lost it all. Ashamed and distraught, "I thought about suicide. I was hurt. I knew I had lost everything that night."

Waggoner joined Gamblers Anonymous. But with a full-time job delivering furniture, a part-time job bagging groceries and a full load at Tacoma Community College, he said, he only had time for a few meetings. But he assured his parents his gambling days were over. Last month, though, he sat down at the blackjack table again—and proceeded to blow his entire bank account.

Fed up, his parents kicked him out of their house in Puyallup, and he moved in with a friend. He vowed he has learned his lesson. Still, he said, the temptations are all around him. "Even when I'm not looking for it, I see it."

Organizations to Contact

Addiction Resource Guide
PO Box 8612, Tarrytown, NY 10591
(914) 725-5151 • fax: (914) 631-8077
e-mail: info@addictionresourceguide.com
Web site: www.addictionresourceguide.com

The Addiction Resource Guide is a comprehensive online directory of addiction treatment facilities, programs, and resources. The Inpatient Treatment Facility directory provides in-depth profiles of treatment facilities. The resources directory is a comprehensive listing of links for professionals and the general public.

Alcoholics Anonymous (A.A.)
Grand Central Station, PO Box 459, New York, NY 10163
(212) 870-3400 • fax: (212) 870-3003
Web site: www.aa.org

Alcoholics Anonymous is a worldwide fellowship of sober alcoholics, whose recovery is based on a twelve-step program. A.A. requires no dues or fees and accepts no outside funds. It is self-supporting through voluntary contributions of members and is not affiliated with any other organization. A.A.'s primary purpose is to carry the A.A. message to the alcoholic. Its publications include the book *Alcoholics Anonymous* (more commonly known as the Big Book) and the pamphlets *A Brief Guide to Alcoholics Anonymous*, *Young People and A.A.*, and *A.A. Traditions—How It Developed*.

American Society of Addiction Medicine (ASAM)
4601 N. Park Ave., Upper Arcade No. 101
Chevy Chase, MD 20815
(301) 656-3920 • fax: (301) 656-3815

e-mail: email@asam.org
Web site: www.asam.org

ASAM is an addiction medicine specialty society dedicated to educating physicians and improving the treatment of individuals suffering from alcoholism and other addictions. In addition, the organization promotes research and prevention of addiction and works for the establishment of addiction medicine as a specialty recognized by the American Board of Medical Specialties. The organization publishes medical texts and a bimonthly newsletter.

Center for Substance Abuse Prevention (CSAP)
National Clearinghouse for Alcohol and
 Drug Information (NCADI)
Rockville, MD 20847
(800) 729-6686 • fax: (301) 468-6433
e-mail: info@health.org
Web site: www.health.org

The CSAP leads U.S. government efforts to prevent alcoholism and other substance abuse problems. Through the NCADI, the center provides the public with a wide variety of information concerning the abuse of alcohol and drugs. Its publications include the bimonthly *Prevention Pipeline*, the booklet *Marijuana: Facts for Teens*, the report *Impaired Driving Among Youth: Trends and Tools for Prevention*, brochures, pamphlets, videotapes, and posters.

Foundation for a Smoke-Free America
PO Box 492028, Los Angeles, CA 90049-0335
(310) 471-4270 • fax: (310) 471-0335
Web site: www.tobaccofree.org

The foundation is dedicated to educating the public about the dangers of tobacco use. It works to prevent teen smoking through school-based educational initiatives and peer-teaching programs. In addition, the foundation produces multimedia presentations for schools and communities and educational videotapes for teens, including *The Truth About Tobacco*.

The Lindesmith Center–Drug
Policy Foundation (TLC-DPF)
4455 Connecticut Ave. NW, Suite B-500

Washington, DC 20008-2328
(202) 537-5005 • fax: (202) 537-3007
e-mail: information@drugpolicy.org
Web site: www.lindesmith.org

The Lindesmith Center–Drug Policy Foundation seeks to educate the public about alternatives to current drug policies regarding issues such as adolescent drug use, policing drug markets, and drug-related incarceration. TLC-DPF also addresses issues of drug policy reform through a variety of projects, including the International Harm Reduction Development (IHRD), a response to increased drug use and HIV transmissions in eastern Europe. The center also publishes fact sheets on topics such as needle and syringe availability and drug education.

Narcotics Anonymous (NA)
World Services Office, PO Box 9999, Van Nuys, CA 91409
(818) 773-9999 • fax: (818) 700-0700

Comprising more than eighteen thousand groups worldwide, Narcotics Anonymous is an organization of recovering drug addicts. Local groups meet regularly to help each other abstain from drugs. NA publishes the monthly *NA Way Magazine* and annual conference reports.

National Center on Addiction and Substance Abuse
at Columbia University (CASA)
633 Third Ave., 19th Fl., New York, NY 10017-6706
(212) 841-5200
Web site: www.casacolumbia.org

CASA is a private, nonprofit organization that works to educate the public about the hazards of chemical dependency. The organization supports treatment as the best way to reduce chemical dependency. It produces publications describing the harmful effects of alcohol and drug addiction and effective ways to address the problem of substance abuse. Its reports include the *National Survey of American Attitudes on Substance Abuse, Research on Drug Courts*, and *So Help Me God: Substance Abuse, Religion and Spirituality*.

National Coalition Against
Legalized Gambling (NCALG)
110 Maryland Ave. NE, Rm. 311, Washington, DC 20002
(800) 664-2680 • fax: (307) 587-8082
e-mail: ncalg@ncalg.org
Web site: www.ncalg.org

NCALG is an antigambling organization that seeks to educate the public, policy makers, and media about the social and economic costs of gambling. On its Web site NCALG provides news of recent legislation and current and archived issues of the NCALG quarterly newsletter.

National Council on Alcoholism and
Drug Dependence (NCADD)
20 Exchange Pl., Suite 2902, New York, NY 10005
(212) 269-7797 • fax: (212) 269-7510
e-mail: national@ncadd.org
Web site: www.ncadd.org

NCADD is a volunteer health organization that helps individuals overcome addictions, develops substance abuse prevention and education programs for youth, and advises the federal government on drug and alcohol policies. It operates the Campaign to Prevent Kids from Drinking. Its publications include brochures and fact sheets, such as the fact sheet "Youth, Alcohol and Other Drugs."

National Council on Problem Gambling (NCPG)
216 G St. NE, Washington, DC 20002
(202) 547-9204 • fax: (202) 547 9206
e-mail: ncpg@ncpgambling.org
Web site: www.ncpgambling.org

The NCPG was established to spread awareness about the problem of pathological gambling and to ensure the availability of treatment and counseling services to problem gamblers and their families. The council sponsors the publication of the *Journal of Gambling Studies* and publishes brochures and fact sheets, including "Adolescent Gambling and Problem Gambling."

National Institute on Alcohol Abuse and Alcoholism (NIAAA)

Willco Bldg., 6000 Executive Blvd., Bethesda, MD 20892-7003
(301) 496-4000
e-mail: niaaaweb-r@exchange.nih.gov
Web site: www.niaaa.nih.gov

As part of the National Institutes of Health, NIAAA supports and conducts biomedical and behavioral research on the causes, consequences, treatment, and prevention of alcoholism and alcohol-related problems. The institute disseminates the findings of this research to the public, researchers, policy makers, and health care providers. The NIAAA publishes pamphlets, reports, the quarterly journal *Alcohol Research & Health*, and *Alcohol Alert* bulletins.

National Institute on Drug Abuse (NIDA)

U.S. Dept. of Health and Human Services
Bethesda, MD 20892
(301) 443-1124
e-mail: information@lists.nida.nih.gov
Web site: www.nida.nih.gov

As part of the National Institutes of Health, NIDA supports and conducts research on drug abuse—including the annual *Monitoring the Future* survey—in order to improve addiction prevention, treatment, and policy efforts. It publishes the bimonthly *NIDA Notes* newsletter and a catalog of research reports and public education materials.

Office of National Drug Control Policy (ONDCP)
Drug Policy Information Clearinghouse
Rockville, MD 20849-6000
(800) 666-3332 • fax: (301) 519-5212
e-mail: ondcp@ncjrs.org
Web site: www.whitehousedrugpolicy.gov

The Office of National Drug Control Policy formulates the federal government's national drug strategy and the president's antidrug policy. It also coordinates the federal agencies responsible for stopping drug trafficking. The ONDCP publishes several reports each year, including *National Drug Control Strategy, 2006* and *Get It Straight! The Facts About Drugs*.

Research Society on Alcoholism (RSA)
4314 Medical Pkwy., Suite 12, Austin, TX 78756
(512) 454-0022 • fax: (512) 454-0812
Web site: www.rsoa.org

The RSA provides a forum for researchers who share common interests in alcoholism. The society's purpose is to promote research on the prevention and treatment of alcoholism. It publishes the journal *Alcoholism: Clinical and Experimental Research* nine times a year as well as the book series Recent Advances in Alcoholism.

Bibliography

Books

Philip Bean and Teresa Nemitz, eds.	*Drug Treatment: What Works?* New York: Routledge, 2004.
Rosalyn Carson-Dewitt and Joseph Weiss, eds.	*Drugs, Alcohol, and Tobacco: Learning About Addictive Behavior.* New York: MacMillan Reference, 2003.
Rod Colvin	*Prescription Drug Addiction: The Hidden Epidemic.* Omaha, NE: Addicus, 2002.
Thomas Cummings et al.	*Futures at Stake: Youth, Gambling, and Society.* Reno: University of Nevada Press, 2003.
Jeffrey Derevensky and Rina Gupta	*Gambling Problems in Youth: Theoretical and Applied Perspectives.* New York: Plenum, 2004.
Carlo DiClemente	*Addiction and Change: How Addictions Develop and How People Recover.* New York: Guilford, 2003.
Mitch Earlywine	*Understanding Marijuana: A New Look at the Scientific Evidence.* New York: Oxford University Press, 2002.
Denise B. Kandel, ed.	*Stages and Pathways of Drug Involvement: Examining the Gateway Hypothesis.* New York: Cambridge University Press, 2002.

Jean Kilbourne — *Deadly Persuasion: Why Women and Girls Must Fight the Addictive Power of Advertising.* New York: Free Press, 1999.

Cynthia Kuhn et al. — *Buzzed: The Straight Facts About the Most Used and Abused Drugs from Alcohol to Ecstasy.* New York: Norton, 1998.

Little Hoover Commission — *For Our Health and Safety: Joining Forces to Defeat Addiction.* Sacramento, CA: Little Hoover Commission, 2003.

Cindy Mogil — *Swallowing a Bitter Pill: How Prescription and Over the Counter Drug Abuse Is Ruining Lives.* Far Hills, NJ: New Horizon, 2001.

Stanton Peele — *Diseasing of America: How We Allowed Recovery Zealots and the Treatment Industry to Convince Us We Are Out of Control.* San Francisco: Jossey-Bass, 1999.

Jeffrey Schaler — *Addiction Is a Choice.* Chicago: Open Court, 2000.

Jacob Sullum — *Saying Yes: In Defense of Drug Use.* New York: Tarcher, 2003.

Joseph Volpicelli and Maia Szalavitz — *Recovery Options: The Complete Guide.* New York: Wiley, 2000.

Koren Zailckas — *Smashed: The Story of a Drunken Girlhood.* New York: Viking, 2005.

Periodicals

American Medical Association "Underage Drinkers' Risk of Brain Damage," *USA Today* magazine, February 2003.

Ross Atkin "Keeping Kids Clean," *Christian Science Monitor*, December 4, 2002.

Harvey Black "Nicotine on the Brain," *Milwaukee Journal Sentinel*, October 23, 2005.

David Borden "The Ultimate Anti-Drug," *Utne*, August 19, 2004.

Benedict Carey "Between Addiction and Abstinence," *New York Times*, May 7, 2006.

Centers for Disease Control and Prevention "Chronic Disease Prevention: At a Glance, Targeting Tobacco Use, the Nation's Leading Cause of Death, 2006." www.cdc.gov/nccdphp/ publications/aag/pdf/ aag_osh2006.pdf.

Susan E. Foster et al. "Alcohol Consumption and Expenditures for Underage Drinking and Adult Excessive Drinking," *Journal of the American Medical Association*, February 2003.

Tom Grey "An Epidemic of Gambling," *Family Voice*, July/August 1999.

Amy Harmon "Young, Assured, and Playing Pharmacist to Friends," *New York Times*, November 16, 2005.

Kathiann M. Kowalski "How Tobacco Ads Target Teens," *Current Health 2*, April/May 2002.

Donna Leinwand "Latest Trend in Drug Abuse: Youths Risk Death for Cough Remedy High," *USA Today*, December 29, 2003.

Davis Masci "Preventing Teen Drug Use," *CQ Researcher*, March 15, 2002.

Jay Mathews "A Feverish Approach to Teenage Drinking," *Washington Post*, March 15, 2005.

Jim McDonough "A Weed by Any Other Name," *Christian Science Monitor*, December 16, 2002.

Siobhan McDonough "Study: Alcohol Ads Reaching Teens," Associated Press, September 24, 2002.

Kathleen McGowan "Addiction: Pay Attention," *Psychology Today*, November/December 2004.

Stanton Peele "The Surprising Truth About Addiction," *Psychology Today*, May/June 2004.

Jeffrey Ressner "When Gambling Becomes Addictive," *Time*, August 1, 2005.

Ted Roberts "I Never Dream of Nicotine," *Ideas on Liberty*, May 2003.

Shari Rudavsky "Recovering Addict Recalls Path to Addiction," *Indianapolis Star*, May 29, 2005.

David Sheff · "My Addicted Son: A Father's Story of Methamphetamine Addiction," *New York Times*, February 6, 2005.

Bill Stronach · "Alcohol Advertising Must Be Curtailed to Change Attitudes to Drinking," *Online Opinion*, July 3, 2003.

Jacob Sullum · "High Road: Marijuana as a 'Gateway' Drug," *Reason*, January 24, 2003.

Jacob Sullum · "H: The Surprising Truth About Heroin and Addiction," *Reason*, June 2003.

Marianne Szegedy-Maszak · "The Worst of All Bets: New Thinking Provides Hope for Gambling Addicts," *New York Times*, May 25, 2005.

Linsey Tanner · "Study Says Many Options for Alcoholics," Associated Press, May 2, 2006.

Index